THE
MAKING OF AMERICA
SERIES

MIAMI BEACH
IN 1920

THE MAKING OF A WINTER RESORT

Bathers at Miami...Jan., 1921.

This photograph shows many people standing or swimming in the Atlantic Ocean, in front of Smith's Casino. Many of the bathing suits are rented, with "Smith" written in big letters across the front.

THE
MAKING OF AMERICA
SERIES

MIAMI BEACH
IN 1920
THE MAKING OF A WINTER RESORT

ABRAHAM D. LAVENDER

ARCADIA

Copyright © 2002 by Abraham D. Lavender.
ISBN 0-7385-2351-8

Published by Arcadia Publishing,
an imprint of Tempus Publishing, Inc.
2 Cumberland Street
Charleston, SC 29401

Printed in Great Britain.

Library of Congress Catalog Card Number: 2001087163

For all general information contact Arcadia Publishing at:
Telephone 843-853-2070
Fax 843-853-0044
E-Mail sales@arcadiapublishing.com

For customer service and orders:
Toll-Free 1-888-313-2665

Visit us on the Internet at http://www.arcadiapublishing.com

FRONT COVER: *The Flamingo Hotel, which opened with an invitation-only party on December 31, 1920, was Miami Beach's first large luxury hotel and helped begin Miami Beach's emergence as America's Greatest Winter Resort. This postcard shows a tea party with dancing on the Biscayne Bay side of the Flamingo.*

CONTENTS

DEDICATION AND ACKNOWLEDGMENTS

I express a special appreciation to my mother, Velma, to whom I dedicate this book. She was born on October 12, 1920, the day after 50 women of Miami Beach were entertained with refreshments, stunts, and dancing at Smith's Casino, the same day the first kindergarten class started at Miami Beach's new Ida M. Fisher Elementary School, and the day before the *Miami Metropolis* cautioned tourists that the clay and sand roads in North Carolina, South Carolina (where she was born), Georgia, and north Florida were difficult to travel and required extreme caution because of heavy rain.

I began research on this book in 1996 and a number of people have helped since then. Most of the voluminous research of the *Miami Herald* and the *Miami Metropolis* was conducted at the Otto G. Richter Library at the University of Miami, so thanks go to the library staff, especially to Eduardo Avella.

Research of Miami Beach's city council minutes and other city records was made possible by the support of Richard Brown, then city clerk of Miami Beach, and a dedicated historian, to whom appreciation is expressed. Thanks go to the staff of the Florida and Genealogy rooms at the Miami-Dade Public Library in downtown Miami and the library staff at Florida International University.

Appreciation is expressed for a Provost/Florida International University Foundation grant, which provided assistance in the summer of 1997.

Appreciation is expressed to Myrna and Seth Bramson for the loan of two special photographs, including the rare photograph of Joe's Stone Crabs Restaurant, from their amazing collection of south Florida memorabilia. Appreciation is expressed to the Historical Museum of Southern Florida, especially to Dawn Hugh, for a number of photographs.

Special appreciation is expressed to Larry Wiggins, who not only assisted me in several specific research questions, but also graciously loaned nearly 30 photographs from his truly impressive collection of south Florida postcards. Seymour Gelber, former mayor of Miami Beach; Robert Parcher, city clerk; Lillian Beauchamp of the city clerk's office; and Richard Brown, former city clerk, helped with photographs from the Miami Beach collection, so thanks go to them. Dr. Paul George is thanked for his comments on the manuscript.

Christine Riley, Sarah Williams, and Mark Berry at Arcadia Publishing were helpful and supportive, and to them go thanks. This book was delayed a year while I underwent treatment for cancer, so a special thanks for Arcadia's patience. A very special thanks to those who made it possible for me to still be here, especially Dr. Michael Ross, Dr. Michael Troner, Dr. Cristina Lopez-Penalver, and their assistants.

The board of directors of the Miami Beach Historical Association, which I serve as president, helps promote a strong interest in Miami Beach history, and so thanks go to the board members, Dr. Judith Berson-Levinson, Tony Brooks, Carolyn Klepser, Stuart Reed, and Commissioner Luis Garcia. Thanks also go to Mayor David Dermer for his interest in Miami Beach history and for his support of the association.

James H. Snowden owned one of Miami Beach's most palatial residences in 1920. The house was used in 1920 for shooting scenes for the movie The Flapper. *The Fontainebleau Hilton Resort at 4441 Collins Avenue now occupies the site.*

PROLOGUE

While there have been several excellent books written on the general history and personalities of the Miami and Miami Beach areas, this book is different. Miami Beach in 1920 presents a year in the life of a little city, the year in which Miami Beach truly began to think of itself as "America's Greatest Winter Resort." As author and historical sociologist, I chose to use the "slice of history" approach, taking a short period of time, but exploring interesting and unusual facts about the daily happenings during that exciting year. This book emphasizes the aspects of the city that were oriented to tourists and the activities that led to the building of America's greatest winter resort.

As a professor of sociology at Florida International University, the state university in Miami, I have approached the topic through sociological eyes, looking at demographic groups, social, economic, and political life, and the lives of people who played important roles. Because of the tourism orientation, heavy emphasis has been put on tourist activities and on the winter residents and visitors who were a large part of life in Miami Beach in 1920.

In order to help give a realistic feeling of the times, I have included some descriptive and revealing phrases in quotation marks and sometimes I have used the terminology of 1920 to help add to the sense of realism. There was strong racism and racial segregation in Florida in 1920, and some of the terminology, although offensive at times and thankfully not used today, reflects the reality of the time.

In 1920, most married women were referred to as "Mrs." followed by the first and last names of their husbands. I have attempted to find and give the women's own first names, and have been successful in most cases. Miami Beach had major restrictions against Jews in 1920 and I have tried to show the extent of this discrimination in different areas of the city. Miami Beach was a new city in 1920, with people from many geographical backgrounds, and I frequently illustrate this diversity by listing places of origin.

There was great enthusiasm in Miami Beach in 1920, and this was frequently illustrated in newspaper articles. Although newspapers are the source of much of the material, I also used letters, city council minutes, unpublished material from the city's archives, verbal and written interviews, genealogical records, census records, city directories, photographs, and published books, articles, and pamphlets in order to give a broader picture.

My love affair with Miami Beach began in the middle 1960s when I first visited the city. After moving to the Miami area in 1977 as a professor, I spent much time in Miami Beach and, since 1989, have been actively involved in the civic and political life of the city. I have gained a better understanding of the city by serving as special assistant to the mayor in the early 1990s, director of a transition team that helped restructure city committees and boards, housing commissioner and vice-chair of the city's Housing Authority, chair of the Homeless Committee, founding president of the Miami Beach Historical Association, a member of the Jewish Museum's Education and Culture Committee, and author of over 17 articles on the historical, ethnic, and political life of the city.

I chose the year 1920 largely for two reasons. First, it was a very important year in the city's life and the real beginning of the city's march to greatness as a winter resort. It was not only the year that the city got its first large, luxurious hotel, it was the year that the causeway opened, the trolley began operating, the city got its first automatic telephone system, first post office and Miami Beach address instead of being a rural route of Miami, first public school, first PTA, and first religious house of worship. Second, it was also important that the city's first census was taken in 1920 and that the 1920 detailed census data was released in 1992, becoming available for in depth research in the following several years.

Imagine yourself in the year 1920 and see what life was like for people in "the exciting little city on the edge of greatness."

ABOUT THE AUTHOR

Dr. Abraham D. Lavender, a native of New Zion, South Carolina, received A.B. and M.A. degrees in psychology from the University of South Carolina, and a Ph.D. in sociology from the University of Maryland in 1972. He has lived in the Miami area since 1977 and is a professor of sociology at Florida International University, the state university in Miami. His previous books include *Black Communities in Transition: Voices from South Florida*, *Jewish Farmers of the Catskills*, *French Huguenots*, *Ethnic Women and Feminist Values*, and *A Coat of Many Colors: Jewish Subcommunities in the United States*. He is the author of over 100 journal articles, research reports, encyclopedia articles, or book reviews.

1. Early History

Before proceeding with the remarkable story of Miami Beach in 1920, let's back up and look in more detail at the past. Native Americans had long lived in the area that would become Miami Beach when, in 1567, a Spanish mission was established to try to Christianize them. The Native Americans, however, had their own religions with which they were satisfied and the mission soon ended without success. As late as the middle 1800s, the area was still inhabited by a few Seminole Native Americans, not descendants of, but successors to, the earlier Tequesta tribe. Various records suggest a few brief occasional visits to the area, but modern interest in development did not begin until the 1870s, when the area was visited by Henry B. Lum and his son Charles Lum of Red Bank, New Jersey.

The area that became Miami Beach was described as having the following:

> A sand ridge running along the ocean side [which] was covered by a tangled mass of sea grapes. The peninsula that would later become an island was a haven for rattlesnakes, mosquitoes, wildcats, raccoons, 'possum, rabbits and bears.[1]

Nonetheless, the Lums, with dreams of starting a coconut plantation, bought several hundred acres of land from the government, going from close to present-day Lincoln Road south to Fisher Island. They returned to New Jersey and interested a group of local investors in the venture. Two men, Ezra Asher Osborn and Elnathan T. Field, both of Middletown, New Jersey, less than 10 miles from Red Bank, were the major investors in a corporation for buying and developing land. Osborn and Field purchased 65 miles of oceanfront land from the government, with breaks going for 100 miles from Cape Florida to north of Jupiter, including all the land in today's Miami Beach north of the Lum property. Bought for just 75¢ to $1.25 an acre, the land had been purchased under provisions of the Great Swamplands Act of 1850, which encouraged development of Florida land.

Beginning in the winter of 1882, Osborn and Field tried to develop a coconut plantation. By 1885, over 300,000 coconut plants from Trinidad, Nicaragua, and Cuba had been planted on their property, including the Miami Beach part.

Workers are shown clearing mangroves in Miami Beach on March 27, 1920. About two-thirds of Miami Beach's current land was originally under water or cleared from mangroves.

Fortunately, on Miami Beach, an old Native American trail meandered north and south among the trees. The trail was widened for the mule teams. Unfortunately, the wild marsh rabbits and rats ate most of the young plants' shoots and the coconut plantation was a failure.

One of the smaller investors in the Osborn-Field project had been John Stiles Collins, also of Middletown, New Jersey. Collins, a friend of Field, had invested $5,000 in the project. In 1896, Collins came to look into his failed investment and to inspect the area. He saw potential, bought Osborn's share of the land, and became Field's partner. In 1907, Collins and Field began clearing massive mangrove roots and scrub palmetto trees to plant an avocado grove, which was 1,000 feet from the Atlantic Ocean, 700 feet wide, and 1 mile long, running north from about present-day Twenty-eighth Street. After a disastrous failure in the summer of 1907 because of salt and spray blowing from the ocean, Field sold his share to Collins, who then became the owner of 1,670 acres of oceanfront land.

Thomas J. Pancoast, Collins's son-in-law from New Jersey, came to Miami Beach in 1912 on behalf of the Collins family to see what the feisty 74-year-old Collins was up to with the family money. Collins had started an avocado grove, which, by 1920, would be advertised as the largest in the world. However, soon after Pancoast's arrival, the two men shared a vision that a city could be developed and, in 1912, they formed the Miami Beach Improvement Company for that purpose.

Meanwhile, in May 1912, two Miami banking brothers, John Newton Lummus and James Edward Lummus, originally from Bronson, Florida, were the major shareholders in the Ocean Beach Realty Company, which purchased about 600 acres of mostly swamp and mangrove land at the southern end of the peninsula, which had once been part of the Lum property. The swamps and mangroves were so thick that an ax was necessary to cut one's way through. Nevertheless, the Lummus brothers planned to develop the land, actually preceding Collins by five months in filing plats for development. The Lummus brothers filed their first plat on July 9, 1912, and Collins filed his first plat on December 11 of that same year.

Since about 1910, people from Miami had been going to Miami Beach by boat to enjoy the shore where, by 1912, there were two casinos (pavilions), Smith's Casino and Hardie's Casino, both at the south end of Miami Beach. Collins and Pancoast realized that future growth depended on connection with the mainland. They also needed transportation for their avocados. In 1911, for example, Collins was shipping about 18 carloads of produce, mostly avocados, "out of the swamps of Miami Beach." In 1911, Collins dug the Collins Canal, connecting his farm and future development lands to Biscayne Bay. In 1912, Collins and Pancoast began building what was advertised as the longest wooden bridge in the world (2.5 miles). The Lummus brothers loaned Collins $25,000 to start the Collins Bridge, but by 1913, Collins did not have enough money left to complete the

The J.N. Lummus family home, built in 1915, was at 1200 Ocean Drive. The house was named "Salubrity," seen written in wrought iron above the sidewalk.

project. Collins and Pancoast had also started building a casino on the ocean side of today's Collins Avenue between Twenty-second and Twenty-third Streets.

Carl G. Fisher, age 38, a supposedly retired multi-millionaire from Indianapolis, Indiana, had recently discovered Miami through his assistant, West Virginia–native John Hale Levi, and had built a home there. He burst upon the scene as Collins was running out of funds and loaned the necessary $50,000 to complete the bridge. Fisher obtained several hundred acres of land between the Lummus brothers to the south and the Collins-Pancoast interests to the north as part of the deal, and he began grandiose plans to build a dream winter playground. Only a few people lived in the area and only a few buildings existed, but things would never be the same after Fisher and the Collins Bridge arrived. Fisher also loaned money to the Lummus brothers to help with the development of their land and, in return, they gave Fisher 105 acres of swampland from Lincoln Road south to Fifteenth Street.

There was skepticism about the dream, however, and growth was slow. A large portion of what would become Miami Beach was still mangrove swamp and was infested not only with rattlesnakes, mosquitoes, and wildcats, but also with rats, crocodiles, and other such animals, who had their own ideas of the good life. Mules had largely been replaced by machines for the roughest mangrove clearing, but in 1920, mules were still used for lighter clearing work and for farming in Miami Beach. Mangrove clearing was rough, but much of the water area in Biscayne Bay between Miami Beach and Miami was only a few feet deep, allowing for relatively easy development. In 1913, J.N. Lummus and Crate Bowen, Fisher's attorney, went to Washington, D.C. to obtain the first government permit for dredging and filling land. The Lummus brothers and Fisher, within a year, had moved 6,000,000 cubic yards of bay bottom onto the mangroves of Miami Beach south of Lincoln Road.

From 1914 to 1928, Fisher would dredge or fill about 2,760 acres of land, adding to the original 1,600 acres of the sandbar, so that about 63 percent of Miami Beach would be positioned on mangrove that had been cleared and filled in or on low land that had been filled. Fisher was well aware of the power of place, of how our surroundings affect us, and he had a grand vision. While the Lummus brothers worked together, and Collins and Pancoast worked together, Fisher's top assistant and confidant was John Hale Levi.

In 1914, to encourage the building of homes, the Lummus brothers gave away 32 lots near the ocean south of Fifteenth Street, today's famous Ocean Drive and SoBe (South Beach). These homes were all completed and occupied by the latter part of 1914. Fisher sold bigger lots for more expensive homes, but the Lummus brothers sold smaller lots at moderate prices to anyone who was white, law-abiding, and could pay the down payment. By 1915, the area had only about 150 residents and real estate sales of the combined three developers—the Lummus brothers, Fisher, and Collins-Pancoast—were only $35,264. Meanwhile, 3 miles across the shallow Biscayne Bay on the mainland, the booming city of Miami, which had a population of 5,471 people in 1910, was growing toward a population of 29,549 just ten years later. Miami Beach did not have a population count in 1910 because it was not a separate area, but the count would have been only a few people.

With the dream still going strong, on the night of March 26, 1915, with a population of only about 150 people, Miami Beach's 33 registered voters (all men) gathered in the Lummus building on the northeast corner of Ocean Drive and Biscayne Street (in front of today's Penrod's) and incorporated the area as the Town of Miami Beach. The town consisted of the Lummus holdings (Ocean Beach Realty Company), the Fisher holdings (Alton Beach Realty Company), and part of the Collins and Pancoast holdings (Miami Beach Improvement Company), going from Government Cut in the south to today's Fontainebleau Hotel in the north. All of the voters lived on the Lummus development except for three, who lived on the Collins development. At that time, none lived on Fisher's property. J.N. Lummus built his own home at 1200 Ocean Drive. Across the street was a beautiful lawn, surrounded by palm trees, and beyond that were the beautiful waves of the Atlantic Ocean.

John Newton Lummus was elected the town's first mayor and served from 1915 to 1918; Thomas J. Pancoast was the second mayor from 1918 to 1920; and Lummus's brother-in-law Thomas E. James was the third mayor from 1920 to 1922. John Newton Lummus Jr., son of the first mayor, nephew of the third, and a champion swimmer, was the fifth mayor, serving from 1926 to 1928. John Hale Levi served on the city council from 1918 until 1947, including five years served as mayor from 1937 to 1941 and 1944 to 1945. Louis F. Snedigar, the fourth mayor, served from 1922 to 1926 and later served two more terms, remaining the city's longest serving mayor ever with eight years and seven months.

On May 21, 1917, a little over two years after becoming a town and with a population of several hundred, by act of the Florida legislature, the town became the City of Miami Beach. In 1918, the Sanborn Insurance Company, in platting the city's buildings, estimated the population to be 500. In January 1920, Miami Beach's first census reported that the population had increased to 644 people. However, research shows that definitely two and probably three people were counted twice, so the population actually was 642 or 641. Economic growth continued, with an assessed property valuation of $244,815 in 1915, increasing to $335,120 in 1916, $647,503 in 1917, $832,745 in 1918, $2,251,600 in 1919, $3,933,700 in 1920, and $5,540,112 in 1921.

During the year 1920, the seams were bursting loose. The city continued to grow greatly through the Roaring Twenties, part of the great Florida land boom, until the bubble burst in 1925, the great hurricane of 1926 flattened the area, and the stock market began to crash in 1929. The setbacks were only temporary, however, and by the 1930s, Miami Beach was on its way to an even greater future.

As 1920 had begun, Miami Beach had only a few small hotels and apartment houses. But, during 1920, the three major hotels made significant changes: the small but luxurious Lincoln Hotel on Lincoln Road had a major expansion; the Breakers Hotel put in new decorations and kitchen equipment and added a tearoom; and Brown's Hotel was redecorated and largely refurnished throughout. New structures, plus additions and renovations to existing ones, were a major part of the city's growth.

Most important to the building of Fisher's dream of Miami Beach as a winter playground was the construction in 1920 of the city's first luxury resort hotel, the 11-story Flamingo Hotel, with 200 rooms, on Biscayne Bay. The Flamingo Hotel had an invitation-only formal dinner and reception on New Year's Eve, December 31, 1920, and opened officially on January 1, 1921.

The Lummus brothers and the Collins interests were major developers of Miami Beach, but it was Fisher who aimed to make Miami Beach the "World's Winter Playground." Fisher poured large amounts of money into developing Miami Beach as a winter-sports playground for the wealthy, with polo, golf, boating, tennis, ladies' horseback riding, deep-sea fishing, and seaplane flying.

In 1920, polo fields were increased and improved. The first international United States–Cuba polo match was held in Miami Beach, with the first game being described as the greatest day in the history of the young city. Two new golf courses were being added or planned to add to the one already existing. Boating regattas and races were heavily publicized with national champions participating.

John Newton "Newt" Lummus Jr. was a champion swimmer and Miami Beach mayor from 1926 until 1928.

This 1924 photo shows Miami Beach's city hall (left) at 609 Collins Avenue and the fire station (right) at 607 Collins Avenue. The fire engine was kept in the opening on the right side.

A new indoor tennis court, described as "large enough in which to drill a battalion," was constructed on Lincoln Road under the supervision of a world champion coach. Miles of bridle paths for horseback riding were built, largely at the encouragement of Jane Fisher. Fishing cruises were a new major attraction, and seaplanes took hotel guests for rides. Fisher brought to Miami Beach many world champion players and coaches in several sports for the benefit of affluent winter visitors. He attracted the best-known polo manager in the United States; the six Nelson golfing brothers, who were the largest professional golfing family in the United States; the famous boat racing champion Gar Wood; and the trainer of the 1913 American Davis Cup in tennis. An impressive aquarium and biological laboratory were being constructed during the year and received extensive publicity in *National Geographic*.

The Miami Beach Casino, owned by Fisher and opened to the public, was converted into the upscale members-only Miami Beach Club, with entertainment for the winter visitors. The Art Center was founded, and plans were made to erect the city's first theater, the Altonia. The Altonia was not completed in 1920 as planned only because so many other construction projects were going on that had higher priorities.

The new County Causeway connecting Miami and Miami Beach opened on February 17, 1920, largely replacing the outdated Collins Bridge. The city's first electric trolley system opened on December 8, 1920, also connecting Miami

Beach to Miami and providing local service with 13 stops within Miami Beach. The opening of the causeway and the trolley brought increasing numbers of daily visitors from Miami, with beach crowds repeatedly being referred to as the largest ever at the beach. Miami Beach hosted one day of the first annual Palm Fete, the first of a long-lasting annual famous parade. Hardie's Casino and Smith's Casino were enlarged to serve the growing crowds throughout the year, and numerous small restaurants and shops opened to serve the growing demand. Joe Weiss, who had begun cooking at Smith's Casino, opened his own restaurant called Joe's in 1920 with his wife, Jennie. This restaurant would become famous as Joe's Stone Crabs, a genuine institution still operating in Miami Beach.

The tremendous growth in real estate sales also reflected tremendous growth in residential development, with several palatial homes, major residential projects, and numerous winter homes and bungalows being built. The need for a business district was recognized and small businesses began to grow. The city's first dairy also opened, but it could not meet the growing city's demand for milk.

As 1920 began, most of the streets in Miami Beach were dirt roads, but the year saw a massive paving project and opening of new streets. The opening of Miami Beach's own electric power plant was another landmark event. The first automatic telephone system was installed and a Western Union Telegraph office opened in the little city.

Miami Beach's city hall in 1920 was a small, two-story building that doubled as the fire department. City Hall was in the north side of the building at 609 Collins Avenue and the fire department was in the south side at 607 Collins Avenue. The new fire truck was kept on the first floor of the fire department. Miami Beach was still a rural route of the Miami post office at the start of 1920, but the new city obtained its own post office in December with an impressive building on Fifth Street (demolished only in 1997). The city now had its own mailing address, giving it a new sense of self-identity. In 1920, Miami Beach also opened its first public elementary school, the Ida M. Fisher Elementary School on Washington Avenue, and the first PTA soon followed. For the first time, Miami Beach's children did not have to travel off the peninsula for an education. A second private school was being prepared for wealthy winter visitors. The first religious institution, a Congregational church, was being built during much of 1920. The parish's first religious service was held in the unfinished structure on March 14, 1920.

As all of these developments show, 1920 was a very important year in Miami Beach's history. The city was on the edge of greatness, with much emphasis being put on becoming the country's greatest winter resort.

2. The Problem of Roads

Getting to (and leaving) Miami Beach was not easy in 1920. Most visitors from the North American continent came by cars, although many came by trains, and a small number came by planes and by ships. However, roads were rough and frequently muddy, trains were overfilled, planes were new and few, and ships were not dependable and limited by their size because of the shallow bay in Miami and Miami Beach.

The southern United States traditionally had objected to financing good roads (or accepting federal help because of their belief in state's rights). This opposition decreased in 1896 when rural free mail delivery was offered and decreased further in the early 1900s as farmers pushed for better roads to market their farm products. With increasing support from tourists, real estate interests, merchants, and auto-related industries, emphasis in many parts of the United States gradually shifted from farm-to-market roads to long-distance business-related and tourist roads.

In 1912, Carl Fisher had become a leading force behind the building of the Lincoln Highway, which stretched from New York City on the Atlantic to the San Francisco area near the Pacific. He also became a leader in the Dixie Highway, a north-south route that would end in Miami. In 1915, after investing heavily in Miami Beach real estate, Fisher crafted a compromise so that the Dixie Highway was not a single route linking the north and south, but rather a complicated network of roads that went through ten states. It would connect both the northeastern United States and the Great Lakes region to Miami Beach. In 1919, after World War I had ended, passenger car production returned to normal and travel to the southern United States increased greatly. Nevertheless, there still were major problems getting through parts of the south.

In Florida, Sidney J. Catts, referred to as the "Cracker Messiah" and governor from 1917 to 1921, supported a road building and improvement project. There had been much criticism of inhumane treatment of prisoners (especially African Americans) both within the prison system and when they were leased out to private individuals. Catts believed that convict labor was cheap for the taxpayers and improved life for convicts. In 1917, the Florida legislature had approved the Convict Lease Act, which provided that state prison doctors would examine all

This photo with Carl Fisher on the left, Claude Matlack, famous local photographer, on the right, and the Atlantic Ocean in the background, was taken on January 31, 1921.

prisoners and grade them according to physical condition and the work they could safely perform. No prisoners could be worked more than 60 hours a week or 11 hours in any one day. The State Road Department had 300 convicts assigned to it and, by July 1918, the department had established five road camps using convicts, with high quality work. This arrangement allowed Florida to provide its share of matching funds and, thereby, receive federal matching funds for roads. As a result, Florida's roads were relatively good, especially when compared to parts of southern Georgia.

Carl Fisher was close to his mother, Ida Graham Fisher, and in a letter to her dated December 19, 1919, he strongly urged her to visit Miami Beach in January 1920. He told her to take a train to Jacksonville and not to take any of the very few boats because they were generally dirty, unsafe, and had bad food. He wrote that he would send a driver, Fred, to Jacksonville to bring her on from there to Miami Beach by car. While today the Miami Beach–Jacksonville drive takes about six or seven hours, Fisher wrote his mother that his driver could be in Jacksonville in a day and a half, and that they could get to Miami Beach in at least two days on the road. His mother soon visited Miami Beach by car.

Fisher had developed his salesmanship as a young boy hawking candy, peanuts, books, and magazines on railroads in Indiana in the glory years of railroads, but he looked to the future and had developed a strong interest and involvement in highways. Despite his intense work for the Lincoln Highway and the Dixie Highway, by 1920, Fisher had lost most of his interest in highway associations because he thought that the American people were not enthusiastic enough about them. Fisher was also a restless person, who was always ready to move on to a new project. A *Miami Metropolis* headline of April 2 proclaimed, "Dixie Highway Opening to Send Many to Miami." Dade County was eager to do its part, but serious construction and financial problems developed and the 1920 headline was premature. The Dixie Highway would not be completed until the late 1920s, but pressure continued for the construction of better roads.

Despite Fisher's preference for Florida roads over ocean boats in 1920, muddy and washed-out roads still frequently presented major problems for drivers trying to get to Miami Beach. Because of problems caused by rain and other adverse weather patterns, there were periodic reports on the conditions of roads. The road from Waycross, Georgia to Jacksonville, Florida, part of the eastern wing of the Dixie Highway, was an unusually bad road. It was also of special concern to Fisher and others because of its crucial link in the chain to Miami Beach. In 1919 and 1920, Fisher was in frequent friendly and business communications with W.T. Anderson, president and editor of the *Macon Daily Telegraph* in Georgia. On November 29, 1919, Fisher wrote Anderson that he had some friends come to

After hundreds of miles over often-muddy dirt roads through several states, tourists finally reached paradise, Fifth Street in Miami Beach, with the Atlantic Ocean, palm trees, and sun at the end of the street. Then, because of the city's popularity, the tourists might have to face traffic congestion at peak periods.

Miami Beach the previous day by the Waycross Route and that they had sat on his porch for an hour and a half, loudly cursing the Waycross-Jacksonville Route and everybody in Georgia.

Anderson wrote Fisher that 50 convicts from the Georgia state prison would build a 21-mile gravel road through sparsely populated Charlton County, in the southeastern sand area of the state, which was "largely afflicted" with the Okefinokee Swamp and did not have a large county road budget. Anderson acknowledged that the road in question was the neck of the funnel for travel through Georgia to Florida and that the road was a bad advertisement for Georgia.

Fisher had offered to pay $5,000 of the cost of building the road as an inducement, but the money was not accepted. Anderson wrote Fisher on January 23, 1920 that "I hope some day to meet you at the half-way point on that road and drink a bottle of champagne enclosed in a solid cake of ice. Do you know where we can get the champagne, I know where we can get the ice?" Fisher, with his characteristic independent spirit and disregard for Prohibition, which had gone into effect a few days earlier, replied with the following to Anderson on January 26:

> I will meet you at any point on that road any day in the year, day or night, and drink that champagne with you, after you get a first-class road between Waycross and Jacksonville, and I will not only furnish the champagne but I will furnish the ice.

Fisher suggested that Anderson move to Miami and take over the *Miami Metropolis*, and he also kidded Anderson about the lot that he had given him in Miami Beach, a lot that was increasing rapidly in value. Fisher wrote that if he had known the lot was going to be so valuable, he would have given him a place in the swamps with mosquitoes.

The working relationship of Anderson and Fisher was very important in improving the Waycross-Jacksonville road, but for 1920, the Waycross-Jacksonville problem, as well as others, was not solved. Although roads in Florida were better than the roads in Georgia, in early February, the stretch of road from St. Augustine to Bunnell, Florida was impassable. The road was taken over by the state highway department, who, using convict labor, made the road passable in one week instead of the three weeks expected. Nonetheless, the road from Jacksonville to Savannah by way of Brunswick was still impassable. In 1920, the ferry at Darien, Georgia had been out of commission since December 1 of the previous year, so there was no way to get from Jacksonville to Savannah by car. Motorists could go through Waycross, Georgia, much out of their way, and get to the Savannah-Augusta road.

In April 1920, there was another notice that the Waycross road was again passable (but rough) after the washout of two bridges. Dade County Commissioner J.C. Baile, who had pushed hard to get the Dade County Causeway completed, drove 784 miles from Dade County to Gainesville, Georgia (about 60 miles northeast of Atlanta) in early June, and reported back that the much-discussed Waycross road was a good road. He wrote that there were other stretches of road between Miami and Gainesville, Georgia that were worse than the infamous Jacksonville-Waycross road, but that he had encountered no mud on his entire trip. Meanwhile, Miami Beach mayor Thomas J. Pancoast and his wife, Katherine, were preparing to ship their automobile from Jacksonville to Baltimore. In mid-July, the mayor and his wife returned to Miami Beach by car, having a "most pleasant" trip all the way, and having only one tire puncture the entire trip. Perhaps because long-distance travel by cars was new and exciting, and perhaps because there still was a small town feeling in Miami Beach, many brief items in the newspapers listed people who were traveling out of town.

While most attention was given to people driving to Miami Beach, there also was a little attention given to motorists who were driving north. One report from Greenville, South Carolina in early June noted that hundreds of motorists from Florida, Georgia, South Carolina, and other southeast states were driving to mountain resorts in the South Carolina–North Carolina area, and that the roads were in splendid condition in Greenville County. The road from Greenville to Asheville, North Carolina was in fine condition except for several bad places. In 1920, Miami Beach had many residents who went north for the summer and surely some of these experienced these Carolina roads.

Mud and washed-out roads and bridges were not the only problem that might be encountered driving to or from Miami Beach in 1920. In August, Mr. and Mrs. C.E. Taylor drove from Jacksonville to Miami, reporting that they had a running fight with mosquitoes from Daytona onward and that they drove all night to escape them. Brief items about local people traveling continued in the newspapers. On August 16, 1920, the *Miami Metropolis* reported that Mr. and Mrs. D.W. Whitman and their son Robert had just returned from a trip, finding the roads "impossible," and, at one place between Waycross and Jacksonville, they had to use 12 oxen before being able to proceed.

Automobiles had become popular so rapidly that providing facilities had not kept up and people frequently would simply stop by a road and set up camp. Some tourists traveled cheaply because they were on limited budgets, some because there were no alternatives, and others "roughed it" for fun and adventure. Nick Wynne writes about the intrepid souls who, "throwing a tent in the back or strapping it on top of the car . . . carrying extra gasoline in 5-gallon cans, plenty of canned food in sacks, and extra tires strapped to the fenders," set out on long trips over hazardous roads.[1] The "Tin-Can Tribe" not only took tents and camping outfits, but sometimes also had folded bedsprings on the running board and cots and bedding piled up anywhere a spot could be made.

On October 1, the *Miami Herald* had shown this situation when it reported on the arrival in Miami Beach of Leslie Combs, his wife, and two children, from Nashville, Tennessee. The Combs family had driven in their 1915 Ford touring car, staying in camping grounds and spending $30 on the trip. Combs reported that the roads were in fair shape, but he was surprised that Miami Beach and

Miami, unlike most cities of any size, did not have camping grounds for travelers. E.G. Sewell, president of the Miami Chamber of Commerce, and some other local leaders had encouraged Miami to build a tent city to take care of the excess winter population that would not be able to find housing. The *Miami Herald* had editorialized that the idea was worth considering, but it had not yet happened. On October 13, the *Herald* reported that plans were underway to provide tent cities on the 130 miles from Vero Beach to Miami. Perhaps the Combs family was a little early.

Miami Beach actually had a tent city of at least ten tents in early February 1920, all well floored and comfortable, on the beach between Smith's Casino and the government reservation. Between 40 and 50 tourists, men, women, and children, lived together as one big family with etiquette and ceremony abandoned. However, these tourists were not part of the "Tin-Can Tribe." They could afford nice hotel rooms if they could find one, but preferred to spend their vacation in a tent by the seashore. In December 1919, attorneys for the estate of Elnathan T. Field, one of the men who tried to establish a coconut plantation in Miami Beach in 1882, had appeared before the Miami Beach City Council to oppose any plans the city might have to establish a tent city. Perhaps this tent city met the approval of Carl Fisher, but tin-can tent cities probably did not fit Fisher's image for Miami Beach.

In October, Mr. and Mrs. William Jennings Bryan arrived in Miami from Asheville, North Carolina. They did not have any car trouble on the 1,000-mile trip, but Mr. Bryan reported that there were some bad roads and that, in one place,

Miami Beach did not have an automobile dealership in 1920, but the A.M. Robbins Automobile Company was one of a number of dealers in Miami. As this January 25, 1920, Miami Herald advertisement shows, the Chandler Six was a relatively expensive automobile, with prices for the six body types ranging from $1,895 to $3,395.

CHANDLER SIX
Famous For Its Marvelous Motor

Chandler Strides into Full Leadership

IF there has ever been any question as to Chandler leadership of the medium-priced fine car field, it is answered now. The great Chandler Six is sweeping its market. It displaces less efficient cars. It steps in to serve those who previously have chosen only high-priced cars. And it pleases everywhere.

From two thousand to three thousand discriminating Americans bought Chandler cars—open and closed—every month this Fall. And at no time has the demand been fully met. Thousands have waited months for their new Chandlers, and have felt repaid for waiting.

Nothing could more clearly show the regard in which America holds the Chandler Six, than the patience with which these thousands *have* waited for weeks and months for their Chandlers. They waited because they knew what they were waiting for—because they knew it was *worth* waiting for.

If You Don't Want to Wait Next Spring, Order Now

SIX SPLENDID BODY TYPES

Seven-Passenger Touring Car, $1895   Four-Passenger Roadster, $1895
Four-Passenger Dispatch Car, $1975
Seven-Passenger Sedan, $1895   Four-Passenger Coupe, $2795   Limousine, $3395
All prices f. o. b. Cleveland

A. M. Robbins Automobile Co.
409-411 Eleventh Street   Phone 52
CHANDLER MOTOR CAR COMPANY, CLEVELAND, O.

they had to wait an hour and a half while trees were cut down and a bridge was built across a creek. Bryan had been the Democratic nominee for president of the United States in 1896, 1900, and 1908, and had encouraged the construction of roads for farmers. Soon, the Bryans announced that they would make Miami their primary home. In 1925, Bryan would gain more fame as the lawyer arguing against evolution in the *Tennessee* v. *John Scopes*, the "Monkey Trial," in Dayton, Tennessee.

The papers noted that Mr. and Mrs. Willis Pickert of Miami Beach were on their way from New York, traveling slowly and enjoying "motor trekking" over roads that were hard and fast. The quality of the roads to Miami varied by weather conditions. A local journalist wrote in November that a typical road had bumps and mud holes in rainy weather and deep and treacherous sand in dry weather.

By late December, twice as many cars as in any previous year were swarming to south Florida, but roads were still a problem. A lengthy article in the *Miami Herald* on road conditions noted that the road from Pinehurst in south-central North Carolina to Augusta, Georgia on the Georgia–South Carolina line, was rough, but that there was no danger of getting stuck. The article asserted that all the road needed was an occasional dragging, but that draggings were not frequent enough. Tourists were informed of the following:

> The roads through Georgia and South Carolina are not what one would
> expect of well-behaved highways, but in Florida the roads are much

This is a view of the Collins Bridge, looking east, in 1920, during a period of light traffic. The wooden two-lane bridge was the only road to Miami Beach until 1920.

better than they have been all summer, and the rest of the way down one can wheel along from 20 to 30 miles an hour, without serious discomfort.[2]

Florida was concerned about its roads and, in April, highway commissioners from throughout Florida met in Miami to discuss the road situation across the state. The chairman of the State Highway Commission spoke in favor of the proposal to tax automobiles by weight.

Good roads were also important for shipping by trucks and, in May 1920, Miami joined over a hundred other cities in observing "Ship-By-Truck and Good Roads Week." Demonstrations, mass meetings, and trains of motor trucks brought attention to the importance of short-distance truck transportation. People in five trucks and two cars went from the Miami area to West Palm Beach to participate in the festivities. Two days later, a motorcade from Jacksonville came to Miami to help boost the local Ship-By-Truck movement. On May 17, a small turnout of county voters overwhelmingly approved a $350,000 road bond proposal for Dade County with a vote of 179 to 21. Miami Beach voters went unanimously for the bond issue by a vote of 11 to 0.

By mid-1920, Dade County had 6,372 automobiles, a number exceeded only by Duval County (Jacksonville) with 8,734 and Hillsborough County (Tampa) with 6,758. The Miami Automotive Dealers' Association met weekly, usually in Miami, but had a banquet each month at Smith's Casino. Partly because of an increase in railroad rates, unusually heavy motor vehicle traffic to the local area was expected in the winter season.

There was also considerable interest in the Old Indian Trails Highway, which extended diagonally across the continent from Vancouver, British Columbia to Miami. The Old Indian Trails Association met in June in St. Petersburg, Florida. I.E. Schilling, who owned a building supply business in Miami Beach and was president of the Miami Motor Club, represented the Miami area. The association proposed to erect 25,000 guideposts along the transcontinental route. Automobile and auto-accessories dealers and real estate agents were major supporters, recognizing the major benefits to their businesses. The association apparently was not very successful and little more was heard of it.

Plans for the Tamiami Trail, from Tampa to Miami, had begun before World War I, but the trail was not yet completed. Captain James F. Jaudon (listed in the 1920 city directory as living in Miami Beach, where his father-in-law R.A. Coachman Sr. was the municipal judge) had been instrumental in starting the project. In 1915, Jaudon realized the need for a hard-surface road across south Florida and, in 1917, he had induced the state legislature to create the Southern Drainage District to which he was appointed as one of three supervisors. Locke T. Highleyman, who owned Star Island by 1920 and soon would complete Palm Island and Hibiscus Island at Miami Beach, was also a supervisor. His construction interests had built the Collins Canal and had taken over the contract to finish the Collins Bridge. While work continued on the Tamiami Trail in 1920, unanticipated costs drastically slowed down construction and the road would not open until April 25, 1927.

Once making it through country roads to the Miami area, tourists then had to get from the mainland to Miami Beach. A large number of Miami residents also wanted to come to Miami Beach for a day or night of fun. As 1920 began, there was only one car route to Miami Beach from downtown Miami. That route ran across what was claimed to be the longest wooden bridge in the world, 2.5 miles long and two narrow lanes wide with 2,100 wood pilings. Miami Beach was still a peninsula in 1920 (it became part of an island in 1925 with the digging of the Haulover Cut), so it was possible to get to the city from the northern end of the peninsula, but it was a long and undeveloped route.

Collins, with the help he had received from the Lummus brothers and Fisher, was able to formally open the bridge on June 12, 1913. A total of 104 automobiles rolled onto the bridge before one came off and, during the afternoon, nearly 200 automobiles crossed the bridge to the other side and returned. Bicycles numbered 145 and about 200 pedestrians walked part of the way across. It was estimated that more than 1,000 people attended the opening.

The short section from Bull (Belle) Isle to Miami Beach was not finished, so people turned around on Bull Isle or took a boat to the Collins Canal. Tolls went into effect on June 13, 1913. Pedestrians and individuals on bicycles paid 5¢, a one-seated auto and driver paid 15¢, and nine other fares applied to different vehicles. Mayor J.W. Watson of Miami predicted that traffic over the bridge would

John S. Collins (center) is surrounded by members of his family. Collins was born December 29, 1837, was 75 when he completed the Collins Bridge in 1913, and died February 28, 1928, seven weeks after his 90th birthday.

The Collins Bridge went from Miami, in the background, through Belle Isle to the Collins Canal, next to Dade Boulevard. This photo was taken before the Venetian Islands and the Venetian Causeway were built.

grow so fast that another bridge, probably larger, would be necessary in 2 or 3 years. In 1914, 1915, and 1916, the Lummus brothers and Fisher paid Collins $2,500 per year so that Collins could reduce the fare to 25¢ per car regardless of the number of passengers in the car. The Lummus brothers and Fisher recognized that the Collins Bridge soon would be outdated and, in 1916, had spearheaded plans for the County Causeway.

As 1920 began, the Collins Bridge still was the main route between Miami and Miami Beach. The first news of the bridge in the new year was an accident on January 3, 1920 when a lumber truck closed in on a Ford runabout car and forced the car through the bridge side. No one was injured, but the car was badly damaged and considerable damage was done to the bridge railing. The management of the bridge claimed that the bridge was being abused by heavy trucks and other vehicles with unauthorized loads, and soon announced that an officer would be posted at the Miami entrance to the bridge. Speeding vehicles were also a problem.

In the meantime, realizing that Collins's wooden bridge was insufficient for the future, J.E. Lummus, J.N. Lummus, and Carl Fisher, as early as 1916, had each donated $2,000 to finance a public $600,000 county bond issue to build a causeway from Thirteenth Street in Miami to Fifth Street in Miami Beach. The bond issue passed by two to one. A group of people from the northern part of the county filed a lawsuit, saying that the entire county should not pay to benefit only Miami Beach. Suits and injunctions held up the work, which finally started in

March 1917 with a planned completion date of October 1, 1918. However, the time schedules for the beginning and completion of the causeway had an uncanny overlap with the United States participation in World War I, which began on April 6, 1917 and ended with the Armistice on November 11, 1918. World War I virtually brought the causeway work to a halt because the use of steel for such purposes was forbidden by the United States government. Construction finally got underway again after the end of the war. The causeway was not completed at the start of 1920, although the end was finally in sight.

In the beginning days of 1920, the Dade County commissioners had taken over the building of the causeway from the contractors in order to complete it sooner, but the county was having problems paying for the causeway construction it had taken over. The commissioners informed Miami that the county might abandon maintenance of the causeway. Miami had won a court case giving it one-half of the special road taxes levied by the county, but the county said that it was as broke as the city was. Because the causeway was located within the city limits of Miami and Miami Beach, the county had the legal right to withdraw its financial support and maintenance. Major road taxes were relatively new and expensive, so different levels of government generally wanted another level to pay.

Although this controversy was going on and construction was behind schedule, many assumed that the causeway would actually open in the near future. Anticipating the opening, real estate hype already had begun in Miami Beach. The causeway draw at the Miami Beach end was closed temporarily on January 16, 1920 for some work to be done and, during the closing, many people took advantage of this first opportunity to walk across the big span and onto the causeway proper. Many locals went practically all the way across and expressed surprise at the magnitude of the structure. Miami Beach installed walks and curbings on Fifth Street from Alton Road to Ocean Drive, preparing for the opening of the causeway. The Alton Beach Realty Company, on January 18, said that Dickens's *A Tale of Two Cities* could be likened to Miami Beach before and after the opening of the causeway. Real estate agents in Miami Beach would eagerly advertise lots near the causeway.

Finger pointing began as the causeway failed to open as planned in mid-January 1920. The county commission had already taken over completion of the causeway from the private company and now it also threatened to take over the oiling of the roads. On February 4, 1920, a local paper reported that the causeway would be opened no later than February 10 and, the next day, the *Miami Herald* extended that opening date to sometime before February 20.

The county commission published an open letter saying that there would be no grand opening because they felt that the wait had been so long that the actual opening itself would be enough of an event without a formal opening. On Sunday, February 15, a headline proclaimed, "Open Causeway Tomorrow at 2." The article, reprinting a notice from the county commission, noted that the causeway was still in the uncompleted condition, but was safe for travel. Actually, the notice from the county commission was dated February 16 and it announced the opening for February 17. The *Miami Daily Metropolis* had eagerly published the article a day too early.

Finally, the causeway was opened, without formal ceremony, on Tuesday, February 17, 1920, promptly at 2 p.m. as planned. Thousands of people were at the opening, and hundreds of cars vied to be the first to cross. The first car crossing was occupied by three county officials, including Dade County commissioner J.C. Baile, who, as the county commissioner in charge of the construction, had pressured the contractor for a promised opening. No official count was kept, but in the few minutes it took to open and close the draw bridge at the Miami Beach end at about 5 p.m., 49 eastbound cars and 54 westbound cars congregated. The estimated cost of the causeway ranged from $675,000 to about $1 million.

County Commissioner Baile also worked hard to beautify the new causeway, although, on June 7, 1920, he was defeated for reelection by Miami Beach's R.A. Coachman Jr. Baile had been one of the partners with the Lummus brothers and some others who had bought most of the southern tip of Miami Beach a few years earlier, but the Lummus brothers had bought out Baile and the other owners.

Problems remained, but Miami Beach was raring to go. The first major event to take place in Miami Beach after the causeway opened was the annual midwinter regatta. Travelers were advised to take the Collins Bridge instead of the causeway due to the heavy traffic of boats and the necessity to keep the causeway open much of the time. Of course, most drivers did not follow this advice.

©1920 by J. N. Chamberlain, Miami, Fla.

MIAMI'S GREAT CAUSEWAY, OVER THREE MILES LONG, MIAMI, FLA.

The opening of the County Causeway on February 17, 1920 was very significant for Miami Beach's future. This photograph was made c. 1921.

Miami Beach police pose in 1921. In the front row, from left to right, are L.A. Jones and Chief Cleff E. Brogdon.

Although the causeway had opened to traffic on February 17, 1920, some work still remained to be done. The question "when will it open?" became "when will it be completed?" as work continued on grading and asphalting. Completion was expected before the next winter season. Trucks were supposed to use the lanes not yet asphalted, but they ignored the signs. Several serious accidents were reported within weeks of the opening. For example, on April 29, 1920, the *Miami Metropolis* reported the following:

> While pedaling his peaceful way homeward from his employment on the track gang of the Beach Electric Company, Luke Thompson, colored, was run down by a Ford and left lying helpless on the causeway last night just this side of Palm island. Passengers in the car following picked Thompson up and carried him to his home.

Becoming a victim of driving was not the only danger. On June 16, 1920, the *Miami Daily Metropolis* reported the following chilling tale of a death by drowning and another near-death:

> The drowning of Eliza Steadman, a negress, and the thrilling rescue of Miss Velma Lyons, an attractive young white woman of about 20 years, from what seemed almost certain death were exciting incidents at the eastern drawbridge on the causeway last night . . . Harvey Lewis of 220

Dann street, who brought in the negress, and Landon Carney of Coconut Grove, who rescued Miss Lyons, are declared by the many witnesses of the rescues to be heroes of the highest rank, plunging into the black water on a particularly dark night with the tide running high, to grapple with drowning women.[3]

Miami Beach officials requested that the Dade County Commission install guard rails on the causeway approaches. Others suggested that life preservers should be stationed at convenient points on both approaches, within the filled-in part of the causeway and on the Collins Bridge. A few days later, one motorcycle rear-ended another cycle. The front vehicle was driven by Miami Beach policeman Andre de Monceaux and the back one was driven by a special police officer for the Alton Beach Realty Company. The rear-ender went to the hospital.

On June 19, the local papers reported that it had become a habit of some of the dancers leaving Hardie's Casino to "leave town like a whirlwind." These "night speeders from Miami who seem to look upon the beach as a glade town and tear up and down the highways with mufflers open, spotlight pricking the night for excitement" were fined $5 when caught. By July 1920, City Marshal Brogdon noted that there was a serious problem with people beginning to drink in Miami and then coming to Miami Beach. Members of the Miami Beach city council suggested to the city judge that a heavier penalty than a $5 fine be imposed for speeding violators. About nine out of ten automobilists crossing the causeway disregarded traffic signs.

The local newspapers frequently reported that Miami Beach officials intended to stop the speeding. Officer Andre de Monceaux, who had been rear-ended, was particularly successful in catching speeders. The speed limit was 25 miles per hour, but one Miami Beach real estate person illustrated the problem when he said that he just naturally stepped on the accelerator when crossing the causeway because the road was so smooth. On Sunday, November 14, 1920, Art Bailey, a new motorcycle officer in Miami Beach, arrested eight speeding drivers on the County Causeway; all eight were from Miami. Two days later, the *Miami Metropolis* noted that "some of them felt pretty sore over having to appear in court, but every one of them will understand hereafter that Miami Beach is not a tank town and that its automobile ordinance grants not more than 25 miles an hour to any visiting automobilists." The fine had climbed by that time to $10.

Electric motors were installed on the drawbridges on the causeway in June and people were waiting for the electric plant being built on the Miami Beach end of the causeway to begin producing power. In mid-August, the county commissioners announced plans to work on the approaches to the causeway, with hopes that traffic would not have to be detoured to the Collins Bridge.

The Gray Line of buses operated by the Ramey-Witherill Company was rerouted from the Collins Bridge to the causeway on August 23, 1920. Passenger rates were 20¢ to any point on the Miami–Miami Beach route, with a 10¢ minimum fare between different Miami Beach stations. The buses circled Miami

Beach from the south end instead of from the north as earlier announced, but Hardie's Casino, near the corner of Ocean Drive and Biscayne Street (South Pointe Drive), continued to be the terminus.

The Miami Beach city council had a lengthy discussion in September 1920 and decided to endorse the proposal of the Dade County commissioners that the north side of the causeway be used for light automobiles and that the south side be used for heavy trucks and hauling. The matter of repairs and other conditions were factors in the decision. The boundary between Miami and Miami Beach still had not been decided, although a committee had been working on the issue since that summer, so signs for regulating traffic had not been installed. Local journalists believed that the police would probably establish a tentative boundary at the Palm Island entrance.

Now that the causeway was built and in use, and more money was available, there was experimentation with which type of trees and shrubs to plant along the causeway to make it more scenic and picturesque. Washington palms were being set out along the southern side of the causeway, close to the road, with coconut palms closer to the water. Beyond them, a row of Australian ("whispering") pines and oleanders, hibiscus, and acalypas were interspersed among the trees. Royal palms had been considered, but there had been problems with these trees near salt water. There were also doubts about the acalypas, but they were being tried anyway because they were considered so beautiful. No trees were planned for the north side of the causeway because of space problems and because the southern side was the one seen from the city.

The causeway, 100 feet wide on the top with two roadways and an electric trolley track, was described by Miami writer E.V. Blackman as one of the greatest and most expensive works of its kind ever undertaken. Despite this superlative, the causeway did not have lighting as 1920 ended, making it "dark as hell." As a result, there were many accidents and some people were hesitant to come to the beach at night. The first big accomplishment of the new Miami Beach Chamber of Commerce in 1921 would be to get lights installed.

Two days after the County Causeway opened, the *Miami Metropolis* asked what would become of the Collins Bridge, saying that the question was of special vital interest to residents of the north end of Miami Beach. The article noted that the government had discussed removal of the bridge, but that the bridge would be permitted to remain if it was kept in thorough repair and if the draws were operated by draw tenders for free and unobstructed passage of vessels.

Residents of the northern end of Miami Beach (then the area around Lincoln Road and Dade Boulevard) particularly wanted the Collins Bridge to remain in operation. John S. Collins lived at 2464 Ocean Drive and his family lived in and owned most of the property in this area. At that time, there were plans to build a chain of islands between Belle Isle and Miami, and to construct the islands so that the Collins Bridge route would pass through the center of each. It also was "reliably stated" that Fisher planned to build an artistic cement and steel bridge from the Flamingo Hotel, then under construction, to Belle Isle. Hotel guests

This photo of planting trees on the County Causeway in 1921 shows Billie Heins, Rose Weiss, Captain Frank Henning, and Thomas J. Pancoast.

would then be able to go from the hotel to Belle Isle, across the bridge connecting Belle Isle and the city, and back down Alton Road toward the hotel, making a loop. A chain of islands and the Venetian Causeway would be built within a few years, but Fisher's plans for an artistic bridge were overly optimistic. Belle Isle, on the other hand, by 1920 was developing as an island of expensive homes. James F. Mathews and, in the early 1920s, J.C. Penney were two of the owners of palatial homes.

Thomas J. Pancoast announced in early April that, despite competition from the causeway, the Collins Bridge still carried much traffic. Preliminary surveys had already begun for the four islands to be built, so it was assumed that the bridge would continue to be useful for some time. In October 1920, Belle Isle interests requested that the county road crossing Belle Isle be relocated, making a semi-circle to the north. The Miami Beach city council implied that it would approve the change when a plat was filed dedicating the road to the public. The road was not curved, but remained straight.

On December 21, 1920, the toll on the Collins Bridge was reduced from 20¢ each way for two-seated automobiles to 15¢ one way and 25¢ round trip. The desire for a shorter route to the golf courses and the baths, and congestion on the Causeway at some hours, influenced the decision to attract more business to the Collins Bridge. The bridge lasted a few more years, being sold to the Biscayne Bay

33

Improvement Association (developer of the Venetian Islands), and was torn down in 1925 to be replaced by the Venetian Causeway, which opened in 1926.

In 1920, with all the talk about the two bridges, plans were continuing to build a trolley (electric streetcar) line along the south side of the causeway. Work continued for months. As soon as the track could be completed, the overhead trolley system was to be installed and all streets crossed by the tracks were to be graded and paved. The Dade County Commission authorized the Miami Beach Electric Company, owned by Fisher, to install transformers and lines for the County Causeway, provided that the company supplied free electric current necessary for the bridges' lighting, signal lights, the bridgetenders' houses, and the draws.

The electric company was rushing, hoping to begin trolley service across the new causeway during the winter season, which began around November. After coming across the causeway from Miami, the trolleys were to go south along Alton Road to First Street, then east to Miami (Washington) Avenue, then north along Miami Avenue and Sheridan Avenue to the canal, west across the canal to Dade Boulevard, and then south on Alton Road to the causeway and back to Miami. Ten cars were to run in both directions, with turn-outs for passing, but some changes were still possible before the opening. There were no plans to go north of Dade Boulevard because there were only a few buildings there. At that time, mangroves were still being cleared and low areas were still being filled in

This photo shows the County Causeway with the Miami Beach Electric Company plant, Star Island to the left, and in the background, Belle Isle to the left and the Flamingo Hotel to the right.

and expanded. Broad Ripple Farm, mostly a dairy farm, was located on Forty-first Street with many cows, but few people were there.

The opening of the causeway and the beginning of the trolley also affected local streets. For example, not much attention had been given to Alton Road before 1920, but with the trolley line opening soon on the road, as well as an expected increase in traffic from the causeway, more concern was expressed by a variety of citizens and businessmen. The Miami Ocean View Company announced that the 8-foot sidewalk it had planned for Alton Road from Fifth Street to Eighth Street would be continued north to Lincoln Road. Alton Road from Fifth Street to the canal at Dade Boulevard was an 100-foot-wide private road, set the entire length with Australian pines, plants, and shrubbery. It was expected soon to become, after Lincoln Road, "the prettiest and most used street at the beach."

Steel trolley poles, 20 feet high, were put along Alton Road in February. By late March, plans were underway to build three stations, or waiting rooms. They were to be at First Street and Miami (Washington) Avenue, Alton Road and Collins Canal, and at the northern terminus of the line. In early May 1920, the Miami Beach Electric Company began accepting job applications and the local papers announced that the trolley should be in full operation during August. Heavy steel rails were being laid so that the rails could also be used for freight and so it would be possible to connect the trolley line with the Florida East Coast Railway in Miami. Many people hoped for a successful rail freight business. Fisher was fervently pushing for a deep water harbor at Miami Beach and *The Miami Metropolis* noted that if Miami Beach did get a deep water harbor, freight could be carried directly to the docks to load into outgoing ships. The railway service, thus, was a part of the leading argument for the Miami Beach harbor.

The investors in the Miami Beach Electric Company admitted that they were not sure that the trolley would be financially successful, mostly because of competition from automobiles. They expected that there would be heavy early morning and evening riding comprised of laborers from Miami who worked in Miami Beach and professionals from Miami Beach who worked in Miami. Efforts would be made to encourage riders at other times because officials expected that Miami Beach would continue to have major growth. Excitement over the anticipated opening of the trolley line was mild compared to that of the causeway, but at least one real estate agent, Clifton Sawyer, encouraged clients to buy property in Miami Beach on the expectation of a rise in value when the trolley line opened.

Fisher certainly was optimistic. Avery C. Smith of Smith's Casino had written Fisher in February asking Fisher to run the trolley down Biscayne Avenue (South Pointe Drive), past Smith's and Hardie's Casinos, so that Smith's customers would not have to walk "so far," especially in the rain. Smith's Casino was on the south side of Biscayne Avenue, where Ocean Drive intersected with Biscayne Avenue, and Hardie's Casino was on the east side of Ocean Drive, just north of Biscayne Avenue. Both casinos were about two blocks from the closest trolley stop. Fisher replied that the short walk was not an inconvenience, that his own casino (the Miami Beach Casino on Collins Avenue between Twenty-second and Twenty-third Streets) was just as far away from a stop and that it seldom rained. In June 1920, Smith wrote Fisher again, and again Fisher turned down Smith's request, writing that there was something wrong with Smith's equipment if he (Smith) could not attract customers one block away from the car line. He further told Smith that he would have five times as much business as before.

The railway company advanced money to Miami Beach to build steel bridges over the Collins Canal at Alton Road and at Twenty-third Street and, in late July 1920, Miami Beach councilman T.E. James held up an agreement until he was assured that the city would own the bridges and that the trolley company could not close them or charge tolls. The city of Miami Beach planned to buy the bridges in the near future. The trolley station at the Collins Canal and Twenty-third Street was part of a larger beautification of the canal. Over $25,000 was spent to make the land along Collins Canal beautiful and to prevent buildings, which were not in harmony with the surroundings, from going up along the canal. The beautification plan went from Indian Creek to Biscayne Bay. At the bridge crossing Alton Road, filling and planting was also underway.

By mid-September, the electric trolley cars were on their way to Miami Beach and the carhouse on the causeway was completed except for pipe fittings, which were being shipped. Tentative plans were made for a formal opening: a group of representatives from Miami Beach would go to Miami in special cars and representatives from Miami would accompany them back to Miami Beach for a tour over the lines, with a few stops and short talks at one stop. The final activity would be an inspection of the power plant and the Wyckoff refrigerating plant, both on the causeway near Miami Beach. Ten trolley cars arrived on September 17, 1920. On October 6, Mr. McDuffie, representing the Miami Beach Electric Company before the Board of County Commissioners, asked the County to surface the street railway tracks on the causeway and repair an abutment at the west drawbridge. The board approved his requests. W.E. Norton, the deputy clerk of the county board and a Miami Beach councilman, was present along with three of the county commissioners. Finally, on November 6, the *Miami Metropolis* reported that the trolley cars would start running in ten days.

November 16, 1920 came and went, and the trolley cars were not running, but on Wednesday, December 8, the Miami Beach part of the trolley line opened. The *Miami Metropolis* noted that local historians should mark the date, December 8, 1920. The short Miami part did not open because the wires and poles were being used for the Palm Fete celebration, a major annual festival that later became the Orange Bowl celebration in Miami. Ellis G. King, the manager, had been training operators (the trainman on a one-man car) and conductors, or motormen (the trainmen on two-men cars), on operating, collecting fares and making change (10¢ to Miami Beach and 5¢ within the city of Miami Beach), and various other duties.

The next day, however, the local newspapers reported that the first electric car had taken a trial spin on its tracks and that the intention was to start regular operation on December 15, 1920. The ten cream-and-red safety cars, as they were called (they actually had terra cotta roofs), were numbered from 101 to 110. Car Number 101 rolled across the viaduct and moved northward along Alton Road for the initial test. Other cars were operated without passengers on Dade Boulevard and Miami (Washington) Avenue. On December 13, 1920, with the Palm Fete over, trolley cars were tested in Miami with extensive cautionary reminders to automobile and truck drivers. It was noted that Miami had been without trolley service so long that motorists had forgotten how dangerous the trolleys and the tracks could be. Miami had a trolley from July 25, 1906 to September 3, 1907, and another battery-operated trolley from December 4, 1915 until October 27, 1919, when a fire destroyed the system. The 1920 Miami Beach trolley would cover only a small area of Miami, and Miami would not get another trolley until January 11, 1922.

While a special caution was given to motorists in Miami, the *Miami Metropolis* also warned motorists in Miami Beach to drive cautiously. Truck drivers were warned not to park their trucks on the right-of-way, automobilists were urged to use care in crossing the tracks, and drivers were warned not to try to beat trolleys at crossings. Drivers were reminded that trolleys had the right-of-way, especially since trolleys were difficult to stop because they weighed approximately 13,500 pounds.

On December 14, 1920, the first trial run, without passengers, was made across the causeway into downtown Miami. A disconnected trolley and a stalled truck caused a delay, but the tracks were found to be in good condition. On the trip to Miami, the *Miami Metropolis* reported that Car Number 103

> started smoothly from her base and gathered momentum as it approached Star island. Ahead as far as the eye could see were two

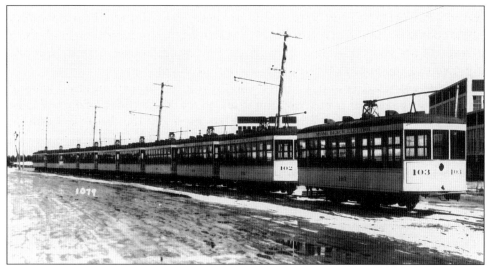

Trolley cars line up awaiting use. Car Number 103 is closest to the photographer.

streaks of rust, the rails of the company. All went well across the causeway. Motorists waved a greeting and good-natured busmen called out some words which were lost in the blare of the gong.[4]

Car Number 103 made a complete round trip from city to city, and the article was complimentary about Miami Beach, saying that the ride in Miami Beach was

> much more interesting than the ride into Miami because of the picturesqueness and beauty of the section through which the car is operated. The full width and beauty of the avenues can be seen and the ride along the edge of the Bay Shore property is unique in trollying.

There were 13 scheduled stops in Miami Beach along Alton Road, Dade Boulevard, Miami (Washington) Avenue, and First Street. Cars coming to and leaving from Miami Beach also made stops at entrances to Star Island and Palm Island.

During the test runs, one fender was torn off a vehicle parked on a street in Miami because the vehicle was parked too close to the track. Other accidents were narrowly avoided and motorists were again cautioned about narrow streets and other conditions. Riders expected that regular service would begin in a few days.

On December 17, 1920, another article reported that the opening was expected at an early date and, finally, it happened the next day. At 11:50 a.m. on Saturday, December 18, the first car left the temporary terminal on Second Street and Miami (Washington) Avenue. The streets in the south end of Miami Beach were being paved and were not finished, so a detour was necessary. After leaving the causeway, cars coming to Miami Beach went up Alton Road, along Dade Boulevard, and south along Miami (Washington) Avenue to Second Street. Cars leaving Miami Beach followed the same route.

On Sunday, December 19, 1920, the first day of real operation, the trolley carried 1,800 or more passengers, with crowds beginning the ride to the beach early in the morning. A number of residents of Miami Beach went in the opposite direction, taking the trolley to church services in Miami. A few months later, the Congregational Community Church would open in Miami Beach and church traffic would go the other way also, but that was not true in 1920. The number of passengers was 1,493 on Monday, December 20; 1,718 on Tuesday; 1,862 on Wednesday; 2,047 on Thursday; 1,841 on Friday; and 2,362 on Saturday, Christmas Day. The first week was a big success, and 4,000 passengers per day were being forecast within a few months. In the afternoon, each car was filled before it started. Afternoon traffic was so heavy that two cars, operating on the schedule of one, were used. It had been demonstrated, after three days of service, that the electric railway system was a success in every detail.

Two days after its launch, on Tuesday, December 21 at 9:45 at night, the first trolley accident occurred on Miami Beach when a Garford bus going east on Lincoln Road hit the trolley car as it was going north on Alton Road. Damage was

Workers are shown paving Eleventh Street. The city's boom required constant road building, paving, and improving.

$200 to the trolley car, but no one was hurt. Only two days earlier, the newspaper had noted that 70 "indestructo" street signs, which had been ordered in October for street intersections, had arrived and were being put up. Most were being put on Miami (Washington) Avenue.

The trolley cars still could not service all of South Beach because the paving and oiling of Alton Road and First Street had blocked some avenues. Councilman John H. Levi reported that the paving contractor, in oiling the pavement, had covered up the groove in the trolley tracks, but soon the route would cover all of that area also. The trolley was off to a great start and would run until October 17, 1939 when it was replaced by buses.

This last problem the trolley workers experienced also illustrated issues that many drivers in Miami Beach had to experience in 1920, whether they were tourists, who had survived the difficult drive from the north, or local residents. Miami Beach's weather had been generally good during 1920, unlike that which those coming south to Miami through Georgia and other states had driven through. Most of Miami Beach's streets were still dirt as 1920 began and major road construction was going on all year. Problems were caused by detours and construction sites as much as by weather. On April 15, 1920, for example, the *Miami Metropolis* reported that if the weather permitted, the contractor expected to have Fifth Street paved and oiled from Alton Road to Ocean Drive. Cement sidewalks, curbing, and gutters had been completed, but final work on the street had been delayed for several weeks because of a shortage of materials. Most streets, however, did not yet have sidewalks and, at a city council meeting on December 1, the mayor suggested that property owners around the newly opened elementary school be required to put in sidewalks within 30 days. On May 5, 1920, the city council approved $124,500 for six road-paving projects, including Alton Road from First Street to Collins Canal. On December 29, 1920, Alton Road was still not completed, but the contractor said that he expected to have the section from Fifth Street to Fifteenth Street completed and opened by New Year's Day. There were already numerous jitneys and buses on the roads and, on November 3, the city council discussed bonding them. Traffic was congested around Smith's and Hardie's Casinos and, on December 15, the council suggested a trial period of one-way streets and 45-degree angle parking.

Miami Beach also had experienced an automobile problem of a different type early in the year. In February, gasoline was running out and a serious "famine" was averted only when two barges with gasoline reached Miami Beach on February 10, 1920. Several weeks later, gas was 30¢ a gallon, the highest it had been in the Miami area, and customers were complaining. There was also an oil shortage, often causing the dredges that were working on land development and roads to shut down in Miami Beach.

There were problems for drivers in Miami Beach in 1920 because so many things were happening and there were so many demands. However, these concerns were minor compared to the problems drivers experienced in getting to Miami Beach and they were a minor price to pay for the city's tremendous growth in tourism as it became the nation's greatest winter resort.

Lanes on the County Causeway were changed at peak times of traffic, sometimes having one-way traffic, to help with congestion. Star Island is faintly visible in the background.

3. On the Rails, On the Water, In the Air

The railroad played a major role in the development of the east coast of Florida. Miami was incorporated as a city in 1896, shortly after Henry Flagler's Florida East Coast (FEC) Railroad reached Miami after gradually extending its line down the coast of Florida. Automobiles and roads were becoming increasingly important in 1920, airplanes and ships were gaining a little in importance, and railroads were losing some importance against these other forms of transportation. Railroads were still vital to the area's growth, however, and to Miami Beach's tourism.

In January 1920, the FEC announced that reservations for leaving Miami would not be accepted after March 15, saying that enough cars might not be available for further reservations. A storm of protests followed from local businessmen because they felt that visitors would feel pressured to leave by March 15, thereby making the tourist season shorter. A Seaboard Air Line traveling passenger agent surveyed the railroad needs, finding a large unmet demand for sleeping cars as well as sufficient railroad cars. So, on March 14, a special train of sleeping cars to New York was begun and the ending date was changed to March 31. Perhaps the whole thing was an overreaction. The *Miami Daily Metropolis* reported that the railroad usually ran full passenger cars well into April, despite announcements to the contrary, and that tourists could stay until early May without problems.

The railroad situation affected items as well as people. There also was a shortage of refrigerated cars for the transport of perishable food to and from Florida. The United States government had also been involved in trying to remedy this potentially very serious problem. A washout of the railroad tracks between Ormond, Florida and Hastings, Florida added to the problem in early February 1920. By the end of February, local growers had lost many thousands of dollars, largely from tomatoes that froze before reaching their destinations.

On December 18, 1917, the national government had taken over operation of all railroads by a proclamation from President Woodrow Wilson, ostensibly for the purpose of unifying rail transportation for World War I. Railroad workers did better economically under government operation than they had done under private ownership, so the American Federation of Labor (AFL) and other labor groups wanted the government to continue operation. With the war over, the railroads were partly returned to private operation on March 1, 1920 and to full operation on September 1. The crisis was supposedly over, but Samuel Gompers, president of the AFL, was in Miami on the first of March and criticized Wilson for "favoring owners over workers." The AFL executive council had three-day meetings in Miami, with William Jennings Bryan being the guest of Gompers at the Hotel McAllister in Miami.

By the middle of the summer of 1920, railroad businessmen were preparing plans for the upcoming winter season. FEC officials, after urging from the president of the Miami Chamber of Commerce in July, were favorable to beginning their winter schedule to south Florida by the first week in November. Local officials argued that the period from November to May should be covered with fast train service and the FEC officials promised to cooperate if they could get help from connecting lines. Jacksonville, Tampa, and Orlando joined in the effort to encourage the railroads to work together.

An extra Pullman car was added from Washington to Miami in mid-September because traffic was already heavier than usual. Indications that Miami and Miami Beach could expect an early and good winter season were received in early October 1920, when trains and boats south-bound from New York reported that they already had heavy bookings. The Bimini Bay Rod and Gun Club was popular among wealthy New Yorkers and many expected it to be a wonderful asset to Florida's southeast coast because of Bimini–Miami/Miami Beach flights. These flights would encourage more people to come to Miami by trains.

New F. E. C. Depot at Miami, Fla.

Miami Beach did not have a railroad station, but the Florida East Coast station in Miami also served Miami Beach.

This train was typical of the Florida East Coast (FEC) trains that came to Miami around 1920.

On November 1, 1920, the FEC put in service the first of its trains for the 1920–1921 winter season, six weeks earlier than the previous year due to the unusually heavy traffic caused by people coming south earlier than in past seasons. Because of customer demand, an extra train was added the first week in November, whereas in the previous winter season, the first extra train was not added until January 7, 1920. Trains were not only for tourists, but also for a few local residents who were only now returning home after spending part of the summer away from Miami Beach. On November 2, 1920, for example, Edith Meloy, who had been in the north two weeks, returned home by train.

By early November, the *Miami Metropolis* pointed out that an unprecedented number of people were coming by automobile, motorcycle, train, steamship, and perhaps even walking. The newspaper said that the fad of pedestrianism [*sic*] was taking hold. By November 9, 1920, all steamship and Pullman car reservations from northern cities to Miami were sold out for at least a month. A successful advertising campaign, the growing popularity of South Florida, and a coal shortage in the north were adding up to the greatest travel ever to Miami Beach and Miami areas.

While most attention was put on tourists coming south on trains, there was also some lesser-known travel to the north during this time period. On August 17, 1921, for example, the *Miami Metropolis* reported that six people, all Polish or Rumanian Jewish illegal immigrants, were captured on the northbound train at 2 a.m. on August 16, 1921. A seventh person was arrested soon afterwards. Federal

This photo depicts the City of Miami *steamship, which was 275 feet long, drew 16 feet of water, and could accommodate 204 passengers.*

immigration officials reported that there was a gigantic plot to smuggle immigrants into the United States by way of Florida. Congress had passed an immigration act, which basically said that Italian Catholic, Eastern European Jewish, and other Central and Eastern European immigration should be stopped so that the white Protestant ambience of the United States could be maintained. Many government officials and citizens believed that these immigrants had entered the United States by ship from either Cuba, the Bahamas, or possibly Central America, and that they had landed at Spanish Harbor, a small village on the FEC line about 30 miles north of Key West. They were believed to be en route to New York City.

While highways and railroads were important to the area, Miami and Miami Beach were, after all, coastal cities. The need for a deep harbor, so that ships could bring tourists as well as supplies for the rapidly growing cities, was a constant political debate. Fisher, who had an intense desire to make Miami Beach a deep harbor city, was very involved in this issue.

As far as Miami Beach was concerned, the most important ship in the news in 1920 was the *City of Miami*. The Cuban-American Steamship Corporation announced early in 1920 that it planned to open its ship line between Miami and Havana around January 20, 1920. The *City of Miami*, a passenger ship that could carry over 200 passengers and would have a berth at the Miami municipal dock, would make the run. Unfortunately, the *City of Miami* would not be in Miami until February 1, 1920 because of labor trouble in Quincy, Massachusetts, where the ship was being repaired. That deadline was missed, but the possibility of direct steamship communication between Miami and Havana was advanced by Colonel Eugenio Silva of the Cuban polo team when the team visited Miami Beach in mid-March. Colonel Silva, like many people in Miami Beach, was enthusiastic about Miami Beach–Havana travel.

By the end of April, plans called for the *City of Miami* and two other boats to operate from Miami, two going between Miami and Havana and one going between Miami and Nassau. Miami Beach was to have a dock of its own and was to play a prominent part in the new venture. Nevertheless, there would be more nerve-shattering delays before the steamer actually got to Miami. The cutting of the channel for the *City of Miami* was also behind schedule and this task proceeded throughout much of the year. Answering charges late in the year that it was behind schedule, the Waldeck-Deal Dredging Company said in mid-November 1920 that the work would be completed in time if the steamship did not come in the next six weeks as planned. One shoal only 16.5 feet deep remained and was being deepened, but all around, the water was approximately 20 feet deep.

Because local officials expected an increase in travel once the *City of Miami* service was inaugurated, the *Miami Metropolis* reported that Señor Miguel Caballero, consul de la Republica de Cuba en Miami, had just returned from a trip to Havana and had said that full passports would be issued to Cuba-bound passengers. The article also noted that Señor Cabellero's two granddaughters had entered St. Catherine's academy as students.

Concerned about the time factor, the *Miami Herald* soon ran an editorial entitled "Deepen the Channel," which strongly urged faster work on the channel so that Miami would not lose the *City of Miami* to another port. The newspaper stated that many people had heard about Havana and wanted to go there. A few days later, the dredge *Manetto*, which had been working in the channel along the causeway, moved down to join the dredge *Norman H. Davis*, which was cleaning out the slip near the Miami Beach end of the causeway in preparation for the *City of Miami*. The expectation was that the mass of sand near the docks would be removed by the two dredges within six weeks so that the *City of Miami* could enter.

As late as December, local concern continued about whether the channel was going to be ready for the arrival of the *City of Miami*. The steamer would be the largest passenger vessel ever to enter the port of Miami. It was 275 feet long, had a beam 42 feet long, and drew 16 feet of water. It had a speed of 18.5 knots (1 knot equals 1 nautical mile per hour). The ship had 102 staterooms and could accommodate a total of 204 passengers.

The *City of Miami* finally left Boston on December 10, 1920 and, on December 15, people waited all day in Miami and Miami Beach for the arrival, amid concerns that there would not be enough water in the cut and channel. Since its beginning, Miami had experienced a shipping problem because Biscayne Bay was very shallow in places and, hence, presented a major challenge to developing a deep-water harbor. Refusing to give up, Henry Flagler had dredged a 12-foot-deep channel from Cape Florida to Miami in 1897. Even in the days before major environmental awareness, dredging was controversial. Some people objected to the mounds of dirt or islands that were formed because they blocked views or interfered with sailing. Intense pressure existed to continue to dig increasingly deeper channels to allow larger cargo and passenger ships to come to the bustling Miami area. In 1902, at the instigation of Henry Flagler, Congress had appropriated money for dredging a 900-foot-wide and 11-foot-deep new ship channel from the Atlantic Ocean to the Miami port. Referred to as Government Cut, this new channel cut through the Miami Beach peninsula near its southern tip and separated today's Fisher Island from the remainder of Miami Beach.

Contingency plans called for the *City of Miami* to lay outside the channel if necessary and lighten its load so that it could begin its run to Havana on Monday, December 20. Unfortunately, on December 18, it was reported that the *City of Miami* had run into a thick snowstorm and was still in New York, but was expected in Miami on December 22 and would sail from Miami to Havana on December 27. Many people were greatly disappointed because they had planned to spend Christmas in Havana, but the delay gave the dredges another week to work on Government Cut and the channel.

In the meantime, the delay of the *City of Miami* also caused changes for another ship, the steamer *Miami*. Almost from *Miami*'s beginning in 1896, the Peninsula and Occidental Steamship Company ships had made the Miami-Bahamas trip. However, the runs had stopped in February 1915 when the *Miami* had run aground off Cape Florida. Now, scheduled to begin in December for the winter season, the same ship was to resume the trip. The *Miami* had stateroom accommodations for 200 passengers, plus room for mail and freight. With a tonnage of 1,741, and drawing 12 feet of water, it would be the largest vessel to enter the harbor in years. It was expected that many winter visitors, who had been traveling directly from New York to Nassau in the Bahamas, would instead come through Miami on the way to and from Nassau. However, because of the problem with the *City of Miami*, the *Miami* was put into emergency service for a Miami–Key West–Havana run on December 17, 1920.

On the Sunday before the *City of Miami* was finally due to arrive, the dredge *Norman H. Davis* was "sucking up thousands of yards of sand" from the turning basin where the *City of Miami* would turn to make its landing at Carl Fisher's completed Peninsula Terminal Company's dock. The ship, without heat and refusing to accept passengers, already had left New York after its forced stop there. Although there still was concern about the landing, the Miami-Havana trip was being advertised as a new itinerary. Miami and Miami Beach were viewed as natural stopover places for people coming from the north on their way to Havana, whether they came by railroad or ship.

On Thursday, December 23, 1920, the *City of Miami* finally arrived. Carl Fisher announced that he had chartered the ship for a cruise to Havana in about a week, scheduled to leave on Wednesday, December 29 and return on Saturday morning, January 1. The cruise was to be a "stag" affair, for men only, and Fisher had invited 200 businessmen, officials, and residents of Miami Beach and Miami to go on the cruise. Fisher expected that there would be a celebration when the ship reached

Havana, with some Cuban government officials being part of the receiving party. Another article disagreed about the departure time, noting that Fisher's party was to leave Havana on Thursday afternoon, December 30, and reach Miami on Friday morning, December 31.

Although Fisher's charter cruise was referred to as the premier trip, on Sunday, December 26, during the time before Fisher's charter cruise was to begin, the *City of Miami* actually left on its first trip to Havana. On board was a party of 25 Dade County schoolteachers who were scheduled to return to Miami on Friday, December 31.

On December 28, the day before the Fisher party was to leave, the *Miami Metropolis* published a list of the "fortunate men" who had been invited. The list, a mixture of Miami and Miami Beach men numbering 142, included James A. Allison, H.S. Bastian, W.E. Brown, John M. Burdine, R.A. Coachman, United States senator A.B. Cummins, H.K.B. Davis, W.C. DeGarmo, F.C. Dickey, Cecil G. Fowler, R.B. Gautier, August Geiger, Dan Hardie, Line Harger, Captain Frank Henning, G.H. Humpage, Mayor Thomas E. James, George R. Kline, C.S. Krom, John H. Levi, J.E. Lummus, former mayor J.N. Lummus, C.R. Meloy, L.L. Mowbray, Lee N. Nelson, W.E. Norton, Norman Pancoast, Russell Pancoast, recent mayor Thomas J. Pancoast, Fred Pine, J.B. Reilly, I.E. Schilling, E.G. Sewell, Frank H. Shutts, Avery C. Smith, Miami Mayor W.P. Smith, F.B. Stoneman, C.W. Tomlinson, and Frank O. Van Deren. The article also noted that not one in a dozen of the invited men from Miami Beach had ever before set out for a foreign land.

Carl Fisher's charter cruise on the *City of Miami* actually left Miami at 5:45 on the afternoon of Wednesday, December 29, 1920. The ship was leaving at low tide,

This picture shows the Miami *steamship. Before the* City of Miami, *the* Miami *had been the largest ship to enter the Miami harbor with a draw of 12 feet and room for 200 passengers.*

the lowest tide in weeks because of a north wind. The ship's officers were concerned that the vessel might go aground trying to cross the bar, so passengers were urged to go forward on the ship to shift the weight. If the ship had gone aground, it would have been stuck until the following morning's high tide, but it successfully hurdled the bar. The men first enjoyed a sumptuous dinner, and Councilman Henry Chase of Miami was elected choral leader. Reflecting the Southern origin of many of the guests, he led his companions through "Old Black Joe" and "other negro melodies." The Ray Manderson Orchestra from the Miami Beach Club was on board to provide music, but received stiff competition Wednesday night from boxing bouts that took place in a makeshift boxing ring that had been assembled on the forward deck. A number of passengers got seasick. Manderson attempted to complete his concert, which had been interrupted by the boxing, but by a "court order" from a judge on board, Manderson was "properly confined below deck and the promised concert [was] not held." Boxing was preferred over orchestra music. The ship made slower speed than expected and did not arrive in Havana until early Thursday afternoon.

Fisher's party was met at the pier by Colonel Eugenio Silva, commandant of Camp Columbia, Cuban Army, and M. Salmon, a prominent businessman, both of whom had been in Miami Beach earlier in the year when they played polo with Fisher. The passengers visited a number of places, including the new polo fields, and agreed that a Miami Beach polo team would be in Havana before Lent.

MIAMI --- HAVANA
Direct Steamship Service
FIRST SAILING, DECEMBER 27TH

New Short Express Route - Overnight Run

Palatial Steamer "CITY OF MIAMI," speed eighteen knots, equipped with oil burning machinery and one hundred and two staterooms, including five parlor suites.

SAILINGS
Lv. Miami, Monday—Wednesday—Friday . . . . . . 5:00 P. M.
Ar. Havana, Tuesday—Thursday—Saturday . . . . 8:00 A. M.
Lv. Havana, Tuesday—Thursday—Saturday . . . . 4:30 P. M.
Ar. Miami, Wednesday—Friday—Sunday . . . . . . 7:00 A. M.

FARES—INCLUDING BERTHS
One way $25.00, war tax $1.00.
Round trip $40.00, war tax $3.00.
Parlor $10.00 extra—Dining Service a la Carte

IMPORTANT
Passengers may travel on passport application and blanks for same can be procured at company's city ticket office, Hotel Halcyon Building, Miami.

HOTELS
Reservations can be made at any:
Raymond-Whitcomb Office—Ask Mr. Foster Office,
American Express Travel Office—Thos. Cook & Son—or

Havana-American Steamship Corporation
HOTEL HALCYON BUILDING
PHONE 1742-R1

The City of Miami *steamer was important for Miami-Havana service. When this advertisement appeared in the* Miami Herald *on December 14, 1920, it said that the first sailing would be December 20. This advertisement, which appeared on December 31, had December 27 as the first sailing date. All other information was the same. (*Miami Herald.*)*

Under the guidance of Elias Cofino, who had lived for four years in Miami, where he had been in the hat business, the tourists saw much of Havana. Cofino also served as the Havana agent for the I.E. Schilling Company in Miami Beach. There was a moratorium because of political and financial turmoil in Cuba, and Cofino "related the distress of the Cubans with all the loquaciousness of the true Cuban," wrote Line Harger of Miami Beach on his report of the trip. Harger marvelled at the fine cars available for rent in Havana, writing that the selection was better than any he had seen in New York, Boston, Washington, or Chicago. He also thought that the chauffeurs were wonderful, that they could "swing around a corner on two wheels and just clear a trolley running at full speed."

Different groups of visitors went to different places, some for pleasure and some on business tours. W.S. Maxwell, secretary of the Miami Motor Club, inspected the streets and traffic patterns in Havana. He concluded that traffic moved too slowly in Miami and also noted the following:

> It would be a good thing to send squads of Miami traffic officers to Havana to study the methods employed there in handling traffic on narrow streets. It is wonderful to see those Cubans keep the machines moving in the busy part of Havana where the streets are narrow. . . . I would like to see Havana traffic rules put in operation in Miami.[1]

Ironically, several decades later, this wish was partly fulfilled as several hundred thousand Cubans moved to Miami to escape Fidel Castro's dictatorship and, like all groups, whether Southerners, New Yorkers, or Europeans, brought their driving patterns with them.

The *City of Miami* left Havana on Thursday night, December 30, 1920, but was delayed in the harbor for several hours because of engine trouble. The 25 schoolteachers who had gone to Havana on the initial trip of the ship came back with the Fisher party and the steamship company arranged a dance for the schoolteachers to which Fisher's guests were invited. Because of the delay, the ship did not arrive back into Miami until 4 p.m. on the afternoon of Friday, December 31. The voyage was a tremendous success, with leaders of Miami Beach and Miami joining hands in aiming for a deep-water port. The subtitle of Harger's report of the trip was "Two Hundred Miamians Return Convinced That Miami Is Destined to Be Great Port and the Gateway to the Tropics."

Breckingridge Long was also a passenger on this historic voyage; he was President Woodrow Wilson's appointee as third assistant secretary of state. Long received many complaints about the time required to obtain passports in Miami, although the passports had not been required when they arrived in Cuba. Long promised to lead a campaign to remove the passport requirement in Miami. Harger, in his report of the trip, wrote that the injustice and costs of requiring passports for a simple and short recreational trip was apparent to all and that the passport requirement was a major barrier in building up a major ship business between Miami and Havana. Long went on to a lengthy career in the United

States State Department and is held responsible by Holocaust scholars for being one of the major officials to prevent European Jews from finding safe haven in the United States during Nazism.

On the last day of 1920, the Havana-American Steamship Corporation advertised the *City of Miami* in the *Miami Herald*, noting that the ship left Miami each Wednesday and Friday at 5 p.m., arrived in Havana the following morning at 8 a.m., left Havana for the trip to Miami that same day at 4:30 p.m., and reached Miami the following morning at 7 a.m. The trip was about 15 hours each way. Fares, including berths, were $25 plus a $1 war tax one way, or $40 plus a $3 war tax for a round trip. Parlors were $10 extra. The steamer was described as palatial and equipped with oil-burning machinery, with a speed of 18 knots.

Fisher had a strong interest in developing better steamship travel between Miami–Miami Beach and the West Indies, especially Havana, Cuba, and thought that the possibilities of short cruises were wonderful. It was largely because of his efforts that the *City of Miami* had been able to get into the harbor. Nonetheless, there was still the deep harbor problem. On March 27, 1920, Fisher had written to James Allison in Indianapolis that he was closing a deal for a big steamship. He further stated that he planned to build a harbor for it to land near the electric power plant on the County Causeway near Miami Beach, since there was no place for the ship to dock because it could not get across Biscayne Bay.

Fisher thought that voters would approve $1.5 million for a harbor, but that it would be a year before the election could be held. He couldn't wait that long, so in typical Fisher fashion, he charged ahead. A few weeks later, he wrote Harold Talbot Jr. in Dayton, Ohio, calling his attention to the terminal property that would be immensely valuable. Fisher wrote that he had so many jobs in progress calling for so much cash that he needed help in financing and asked Talbot to talk to some of his associates. A couple of weeks later, Fisher expressed his delight that Talbot was coming in on the steamship company and wrote that there were thousands of people with money and "no place to go" who would make steamship travel a great success.

The spoil banks that were created with the dredged-up dirt of Government Cut became Dodge Island and Lummus Island. Fisher Island, about 30 acres when Carl Fisher bought it in 1919, grew by fill and wave action to about 200 acres. Fisher needed the island as part of his deep harbor plans.

Early in 1920, a port commission was appointed with two members from Miami, Mayor W.P. Smith and Councilman B.R. Hunter, and three members from Miami Beach: Fisher, Mayor T.J. Pancoast, and Councilman W.E. Brown, an engineer. Fisher was proposing that Miami buy the necessary land at Miami Beach and develop this "outer harbor" for large freighters, while continuing to use the channel leading to the Miami municipal docks for smaller boats. Fisher and his associates wrote that they owned the land, but that they would sell the land to Miami at cost, which would give Miami control of the terminal. Fisher felt that his plan to have a terminal adjoining Norris Cut (between the southern side of Fisher Island and the northern side of Virginia Key) with harbor and piers would help the Miami area obtain a much needed deep water port five years earlier than under any other plans.

Fisher released blueprints of his plans. The *Miami Herald*, referring to Miami, reported the following:

> The benefits to the city are not at once apparent. However, it is obvious to all business men that the shipping facilities in the city are not adequate for the routine needs of the present and that the future needs can only be met with a farseeing plan. With extensive docking facilities such as are proposed by Mr. Fisher, there will be no limit to the growth of Miami.[2]

Interestingly, Fisher had written James Deering in August 1919, informing him that he had just purchased 32 acres of land adjoining the causeway and the 30-acre island immediately south of the harbor entrance. The price for the island was reported as $42,000. Fisher wrote that he proposed to add another 48 acres of fill to the island and suggested to Deering that Virginia Key and Cape Florida (Key Biscayne) could be connected to the mainland with a drawbridge. He also suggested the following to Deering:

> If you were the owner of Virginia Key you could put a bridge across Norris Cut and another bridge across Bears Cut, which would give you

The Clyde Steamship Company competed for business from visitors returning north. (Miami Herald.)

GOING NORTH?

If you intend going to New York it would be greatly to your advantage to stop a minute and make comparison of fares via CLYDE LINE with the fares of other routes. It will take but little figuring to quickly establish the saving when it is considered the steamship ticket includes, not only transportation, but meals and stateroom accommodations during the three days the trip consumes—three days of genuine health giving rest with all the comforts and every convenience one may find in the finest hotels. You will find there is a difference, quite a difference in dollars and cents

The invigorating salt air will create an appetite you never thought possible and as our chefs are well trained in the art of giving full satisfaction to the most exacting, you will welcome the call to meals. A stroll around deck—nine times around makes a mile—gives you an opportunity for exercise and if you prefer lounging indoors, the Smoking Room or the Music Room with its large comfortable chairs will prove most inviting.

FARE INCLUDING MEALS AND BERTH **$39.46** INCLUDING WAR TAX

There are staterooms larger in size, preferred location, etc., some with connecting private lavatory, others with brass bedsteads and connecting private bath for which an additional charge is made.

SAILINGS EVERY TUESDAY, THURSDAY AND SATURDAY AT 2:00 P. M.

CLYDE STEAMSHIP COMPANY
Passenger Department   Jacksonville, Florida

Racing boats are shown on the Biscayne Bay (west) side of the Flamingo Hotel. The annual regatta was a major event in Miami Beach, with the date being flexible in order to accommodate special events.

a boulevard entrance to Cape Florida property. . . . it is only a question of three or four years until there is going to be a very great demand for large blocks of Ocean front property, particularly that property which has been filled and is practically rid of mosquitos. You may not be at all interested in the further development of Cape Florida but it is a wonderful piece of property and with the proper boulevard connections to the mainland could be made to show some very handsome profits.[3]

Nothing came of Fisher's grandiose suggestions to link the islands by bridges, but he continued to push the idea of an outer harbor while receiving fervent opposition from Miami. Meanwhile, other work continued. In mid-January 1920, a dredging company completed cutting off the north and south points of the west end of the government canal in order to make the cut a uniform 1,000 feet wide. The ship channel, 300 feet wide, was not disturbed.

Work also was continuing on extending the jetties of Government Cut 500 feet seaward and revetting (facing the embankment with masonry) the shore at the west end of the channel. It was thought that the jetties would keep the bar clear and perhaps even cause a deepening of the water. But, the dredging company working on the unit went into receivership. A number of rough weather days and a shortage of granite further delayed work on the jetties. But, in late April the local papers reported that both the cut and the jetties would be completed in six more months.

Fisher continued his fervent efforts for a deeper harbor and clearly gave his attitudes toward improvement and taxes. On March 10, 1920, the *Miami Daily*

Metropolis reported his talk with the newspaper on the front page. Fisher stated that the people interested in beach development were willing to pay whatever taxes were necessary, and that

> a few hundred thousand dollars is paltry when the benefits are considered. . . . It is a disgrace that Miami should have nothing better to offer as an encouragement to shipping. Here the money for bay improvement has been spent out in driblets, without any comprehensive plan . . . I want to see Miami do things in a big way, commensurate with the destiny of the city. . . . Clear away the mud and filth now in the bay and deepen the water right up to the bulkheads. Keep the water clear and on the move. Make the bay front park as large as possible and fill it with attractions . . . That is our policy for Miami Beach and we wish nothing less for the city of Miami.[4]

The seriousness of the shipping problem continued. On April 1, the Rotary Club asked the Miami City Council to speed up the clearing of the channel to 18 feet. Docks were also in short supply. Twenty vessels were tied up three tiers deep, waiting for accommodations at the Miami municipal dock, and others had been turned away. The urgent increased need for docks was shown by noting that 255 boats entered the port of Miami in January, February, and March 1920, while comparable numbers were 59 for 1919 and 38 for 1918. In April, Fisher announced that work would begin early in May to dredge a slip 500 feet long, 300 feet wide, and 18 feet deep near the east viaduct of the causeway, adjoining the site of his new electric powerhouse.

As all of this was unfolding, the Pilkington Boatyard on the bay side of Miami Beach had failed and rumors started that the site would be resurrected by James A. Allison as a shipyard. The closest place for major ship repairs was Jacksonville or Key West, so excitement was high with expectations of the shipyard opening by the next season. A little later, Miami Beach asked the war department to establish a harbor line along the bay front, for the United States engineering office at the time had already designated a harbor line along the shore side of Miami Beach. No dock or slip could be built further inland than the harbor line. The Allison shipyard in Miami Beach did begin plans to build barges for local transportation of construction supplies. Three massive barges (24 feet wide by 50 to 60 feet long) had already been built at the dock near the under-construction Flamingo Hotel.

Work began in July on deepening the bay to 18 feet for the Miami Beach Electric Company docks. Along with other work, it was expected that the south end of Miami Beach would soon have a great commercial development unequaled in Florida. In October, the Peninsula Terminal Company of Miami Beach (a Carl Fisher Corporation) received a permit to build a levee and bulkhead on the south side of Government Cut, 300 feet south of the old cut and parallel to it. A 125-acre island would be built paralleling the south side and would be available to the port of Miami for warehouses, storage yards, and other terminal facilities. Much of the bay, which was planned for filling, was actually covered with only 1 foot of water.

In September 1920, the city of Miami claimed the island in Biscayne Bay near the eastern end of the ship channel, the land on which Carl Fisher's interests were erecting large industrial works. Two large oil tanks and a cold storage plant had already been built, and a portion of the power plant of the Miami Beach Electric Company and the car barns for the Miami Beach trolley were being erected. The land had been deeded to the city of Miami five years earlier. The deed had a clause that it could not be sold and could be used only for city purposes. Otherwise, it was supposed to revert to the state of Florida, but the dock commissioner said that it could be rented to Carl Fisher or someone else. Fisher also had a deed, but the city of Miami's deed preceded his own. The dock commissioner, E.L. Brady, asked Redmond B. Gautier, former city attorney for Miami who was finishing his service as city attorney for Miami Beach, for his opinion, and Gautier told Brady about the Miami deed being on file in the courthouse in Miami.

Miami was firm in its opposition to a bridge being built over the channel. However, Fisher had moved on from his idea about bridges and now viewed this as a non-issue since lighterage (the use of lighters or barges in loading and unloading ships, and in transporting goods for short distances) was thought more feasible. These changes would tie into Miami's hopes for a deeper harbor. E.G. Sewell, president of the Miami Chamber of Commerce, left for Washington to further argue Miami's case for a deeper and wider channel. Sewell carried with him a study of the amount of tonnage passing through the ship channel and what was expected if the national war department made the channel wider and deeper.

On December 27, 1920, the newspaper reported that Carl Fisher's Peninsula Terminal Company was receiving its permit to develop a harbor south of the channel, following September hearings at Smith's Casino in Miami Beach. A 300-acre island would be the result, with a system of lighterage operating to the terminal docks and Miami, and probably a ferry crossing the channel. Many people even dreamed of a future railway from Miami to the new island, connecting large warehouses and docks for ships from all over the world. Tentative plans had been approved by marine experts for 20 feet of deep water within the harbor, with plans to then increase the depth to 25 feet. Plans were being formed to begin work on the project after January 1, 1921, which would be second to none for Miami Beach developers.

Henry H. Read, compiler of "Read's Waterways," was in Miami Beach on December 15, 1920, and wrote that Miami Beach could be one of the greatest, if not the greatest, port on the Florida coast because of its ability to enlarge and improve its waterfront within the harbor, its natural location, and its enterprise. He called Miami Beach "the Diamond Port" because the current development had the outline of a diamond.

By early 1921, there was a well-defined movement to give Miami a deep-water channel from the municipal docks to the ocean at a uniform depth of 25 feet. In April 1921, Fisher wrote Frank Shutts of Miami, saying that the electric light plant

Dredges were a major part of filling in land and in digging the deep-water channel. Dredges were working restlessly in 1920 to create a deeper harbor for Miami and Miami Beach.

and electric railway were closely tied to the issue of a deep-water harbor for ships. Fisher argued that something had to be done if Miami was to get a deep water harbor, and that both Miami and Miami Beach should try to end the animosity and contention between the two cities. He offered to sell the trolley line, electric plant, and 2,500 feet (11 acres) of bulkhead to the county and Miami to speed the process of getting a deep-water harbor. However, Fisher's wishes for Miami Beach to have the deep-water harbor were not fulfilled, one of the most disappointing of his rare failures. Opposition from the city of Miami was too great for even Carl Fisher to overcome.

While the vast majority of the attention in 1920 went to the *City of Miami*, other ships received some publicity. For example, the *Berry Islands*, a steamer scheduled for passenger and freight transportation between Miami and Nassau, was ordered early in January 1920 to temporarily suspend its Miami-Nassau run in order to meet the immediate need for steamer trips twice a week between Miami and Bimini. The *Bellymena*, the steamer that was scheduled for the Miami-Bimini route, was stuck in Baltimore because a severe freeze had burst pipes. The *Berry Islands* was to substitute until the *Bellymena* returned. Despite Miami Beach's generally good weather, it was still affected by bad weather elsewhere, and smaller ships were also a part of the city's life.

While highways, railroads, and ships were of great importance to Miami Beach in 1920, airplanes were just beginning to be a factor in long-distance travel. The first powered airplane flights in history had been made only 17 years earlier, on December 17, 1903 at Kitty Hawk, North Carolina by brothers Wilbur and Orville Wright. Their flights were met with indifference, but by 1920, the future of airplanes was clear. With his usual foresight, Fisher saw the potential early on.

55

During the Mid-winter Regatta with speedboats, airplanes also performed for spectators. Within a few years, residents were complaining about the noise, and local flights were decreased.

The year 1920 would become important for airplanes in the Miami area. An Aero Limited hydroairplane, stationed at Elser Pier in downtown Miami and piloted by George Cobb, flew in April from Miami to Atlantic City, New Jersey in 16 hours and 25 minutes, with 5 stops en route. The two passengers, Lincoln G. Valentine of New York and Modesto Martinez of Costa Rica, were investigating the commercial possibilities of hydroairplanes. The first international hydroairplane flight carrying commercial freight took place on April 16, 1920 from Miami to Nassau. The freight consisted of diving suits, "worth a most princely sum," for the Selznick Pictures Corporation, which was then working out of Miami.

The first "non-stop" airplane flight from Miami to New York City took place on April 30, 1920. The *Miami Herald* carried a headline across the entire top of its front page, noting that items being transported on the flight included that day's edition of the newspapers. The airplane, named *Miss Miami*, was a hydroairplane of Aero Limited, Inc. and made the 1,539-mile flight in 14 hours and 35 minutes flying time. It had left at about 3 a.m. and reached New York City at 7:35 p.m (8:35 p.m. in New York because of daylight savings time). The plane stopped in Morehead City, North Carolina for 1 hour and 45 minutes to refuel, so technically it was not a non-stop flight, but such trivial matters could not overshadow the overall accomplishment. The hydroairplane picked up flashlight signs and landed in the Hudson River near Eighty-sixth Street in front of the Columbia Yacht Club. Most of the flight from Virginia to New York City was in a driving rainstorm. The pilots flew at about 500 feet high, with an average speed of about 90 miles per hour. Because the plane stopped to refuel, it did not break the non-stop flying record, but it was the longest distance known to have been flown in one day. Miami and Miami Beach were hopeful that this was the beginning of regular non-stop flights to and from New York. Few people probably realized the tremendous importance airplanes would play in developing Miami as an international city and Miami Beach as an internationally known tourist city.

Although the Miami–New York non-stop flight on April 30 was the biggest air travel headline grabber in 1920, commercial aviation was one of the main topics throughout the year. On February 29, businessman William M. Fleischmann made news when he returned from Tampa to Miami in less than 6 hours in a Curtiss Standard plane, counting stopping in Arcadia (75 miles south of Tampa) for a short time to stretch his legs. Miami had the distinction of having the first international overseas line, to Nassau and Havana. The Aero Limited covered routes from Miami and Miami Beach to Bimini, Nassau, Key West, Havana, and Palm Beach, as well as small pleasure hops around the bay. Bimini was the closest "wet" spot to Miami Beach and was a major source of alcohol after Prohibition went into effect in the United States in early 1920. Cuba was also a "wet" spot. On the first day of 1920, the *Miami Herald* ran an article on the planned building of a great gambling resort near Santiago, Cuba.

The *Big Fish*, the largest passenger-carrying airplane in the United States, made news with flights to Bimini. On April 13, the *Miami Herald*, reflecting the novelty of flying in 1920, listed by individual names over 150 people who had flown to Bimini in the few preceding weeks. Included among the flyers were N.B.T. Roney (who would soon develop Roney Plaza), Carl and Jane Fisher, and Louis Snedigar (who, two years later, would become the city's fourth mayor). The *Big Fish*, with 12 passengers, made a record trip in April from Bimini to Biscayne Bay in 38 minutes. Plans were to keep the *Big Fish* in Miami all summer if there was enough business. The local papers celebrated the view of Miami and Miami Beach from the air, so the *Big Fish* was also used for short beach hops.

The *Miami Herald* noted that Miami led all other cities in the United States in the new aerial transportation, primarily due to the large number of people flying to Bimini on the American Trans-Oceanic Company's planes. "The latest method of transportation" was called upon in mid-May for another use. P.J. Dolier, a wealthy New York businessman, apparently could not get out of Havana for 30 days because of a congestion of transportation facilities from Havana to Key West, so he chartered an airplane.

In September, an executive order announced that neither a passport nor permission to depart from the United States, except for Russians and hostile citizens, would be required for travel to Bimini. It was thought that the order would have the effect of opening the Nassau hotels and of influencing the Peninsular and Occidental Steamship Company (P&O) to run a first-class boat line from Miami to the islands. The P&O was a subsidiary of the FEC Railway Company, which also operated hostelries on the islands. Immigrants from Russia, largely Jewish, were treated differently because they were suspected of political radicalism.

The *Big Fish* seaplane, which had made news earlier in the year with its Miami-Bimini flights, made big news again in October 1920 when it made a New York-to-Miami flight in a flying time of 14 hours and 10 minutes. Two stops, in Norfolk, Virginia and Parris Island, South Carolina, added to the time. The seaplane could carry 16 passengers and light baggage. The plane, after arriving in Miami, began flights between Miami and the Bimini Bay Rod and Gun Club.

As noted earlier, Carl Fisher was enthusiastic about the future of airplanes. He had started working with the Aero Club of America to initiate a Pan-American Aerial Derby. He planned for the airplanes to start in Miami, then fly to Cuba, Guatemala, Panama, Colombia, Ecuador, Peru, Chile, Argentina, Uruguay, Brazil, Guinea, Venezuela, Puerto Rico, and Haiti, and then back to Cuba and Miami. Fisher wrote that airplane transportation was coming fast and that Miami had a golden opportunity to become important in the early stages of air travel.

The relative importance of highways, railroads, ships, and airplanes would keep changing in the future, but all would continue to play an important role in Miami Beach's fame.

Bimini Bay Rod and Gun Club

Bimini   Bahama Islands

45 Miles East of Miami.

New Sportsman's Paradise and Family Club.

The big club house is now ready for members and guests and our friends.

One full week of special sporting events, commencing Monday, December 13th.

Two big twin motored seaplanes daily.

Big fast passenger boat Tuesday.

Wireless telegraph and telephone service.

For rooms, fishing boats, seaplane and boat transportation, memberships and guest privileges, apply to

Bimini Bay Rod and Gun Club

Hotel Halcyon Bldg.   Phone 290.

The Bimini Bay Rod and Gun Club was popular and frequent trips were taken between Miami, Miami Beach, and Bimini. Prohibition increased Bimini's popularity. (Miami Metropolis.)

4. MEDIA AND ARTS

Miami Beach did not have its own newspaper in 1920, but it was well served by the two newspapers published in Miami, the *Miami Metropolis* and the *Miami Herald*, both of which cost 5¢ daily that year. The *Miami Metropolis* (also published as the *Miami Daily Metropolis* and the *Weekly Miami Metropolis*) had begun in 1896 with support from Henry Flagler. The newspaper was critical of some of Flagler's investments but carefully respected his power. However, in 1905, Bobo Dean became owner of the newspaper and lashed out against the control exercised by Flagler's railroad monopoly. In 1923, the *Metropolis* would be purchased by former Ohio governor (and Democratic candidate for President in 1920) James M. Cox and was published as the *Miami News* until it ceased publication on December 31, 1988.

In 1903, the *Miami Evening Record* began publishing six days a week, and recognized Flagler's power in both economic and social circles. In 1907, it bought the young *Miami Morning News* and became the *Morning News*. It fell into bankruptcy in 1909 and Frank Shutts, a lawyer who was handling the bankruptcy, convinced Flagler to buy the newspaper. On December 1, 1910, Shutts began publishing the newspaper as the *Miami Herald*. Flagler died on May 20, 1913, but the railroad interests remained influential throughout the area. In 1920, Dean remained as editor of the *Miami Metropolis* and Shutts remained as publisher of the *Miami Herald*.

Fisher wrote Shutts on January 2, apologizing for causing Shutts "so much trouble," but suggesting that Shutts get rid of "the damned fool" who had put something in the newspaper that had upset Fisher. No copies exist for the apparent day in which the article appeared, and no Fisher correspondence explaining the incident can be found. The incident suggests that Fisher did not like a certain criticism and that perhaps he attempted to influence the newspaper's reporting. In March, Mr. and Mrs. Shutts made the news when they went to Fisher's Miami Beach Casino for dancing after the yachtsman ball, where the regatta winners were recognized.

As an attorney, Shutts represented James H. Snowden when Snowden successfully opposed Indian Creek being renamed Flamingo Bay. Shutts apparently had been misled into believing that Fisher had nothing to do with the attempt to change the area's name. In December, Shutts was acting as president of the South Atlantic Telephone and Telegraph Company when the company connected about 400 telephones in Miami Beach, including 200 rooms in Fisher's Flamingo Hotel and 60 rooms in Fisher's Lincoln Hotel. Shutts turned on the switch that made the telephone connections and even made the first telephone call. From December 29 to 31, 1920, Shutts, along with about 150 local leaders, was one of Fisher's celebrated guests on the cruise to Havana. It appears that Fisher and Shutts had frequent interactions.

Bobo Dean was also on the cruise to Havana, but he did not seem to have much significant interaction with Fisher. Nevertheless, the *Metropolis* as well as the *Herald* gave much favorable attention to Miami Beach during the year. It appears that Fisher was closer to Shutts and the *Herald*'s viewpoint on the controversial Prohibition issue, and Prohibition was an extremely personal issue to Fisher. As noted earlier, Fisher, perhaps jokingly and perhaps not, had encouraged W.T. Anderson from Macon, Georgia, with whom Fisher was cooperating in trying to get better roads in Georgia, to move to Miami Beach and become the *Metropolis* editor.

The *Metropolis*, under Dean, was supportive of Prohibition and gave significant coverage to attempts to stop bootlegging in Dade County. It was a reporter called "Madge" from the *Metropolis* who exposed the "supposedly unknown" Jungle Inn on March 11, 1920. The *Metropolis*, under the headline "Mayor Delivers Sermon to the Police Force on Booze and Law," reprinted much of the Miami mayor's strong condemnation of red wine and other alcohol. In the election of 1920, Redmond B. Gautier, Miami Beach's city attorney, and others accused Dean of being behind the Republican movement in Dade County. The *Miami Daily Metropolis* frequently gave negative publicity to those who were perceived as not supporting Prohibition.

Nationwide, the Republican candidate Harding received 60 percent of the vote, while the Democratic candidate Cox received 34 percent. In Florida, Cox received 62 percent to Harding's 32 percent. In Dade County, Cox won by a slightly smaller margin and, in Miami Beach with 229 registered voters, Harding actually won with 74 votes (53.6 percent) to Cox's 64 votes (46.4 percent). Politically, Miami Beach was different from Miami and even more so from Florida. However, Miami Beach's vote probably had little to do with Prohibition, but instead reflected the backgrounds of the voters of Miami Beach. Florida was the birthplace of 20 voters and their backgrounds before Florida are unknown. Of 87 voters, for whom a birthplace other than Florida is known, only 12 were born in the South and 8 in border states. Northeastern states accounted for 26 voters and Great Lakes states accounted for 27. Five voters were born in the Midwest and nine voters were foreign born.

Different from the *Metropolis*, the *Miami Herald* had extra large letters for its headline when an officer from the department of justice stopped the car of a dentist from Wildwood, Florida, who was coming to Miami with his wife and two delegates to the state dental convention. He also had invested heavily in Miami real estate on previous visits. The officer had blocked the road and searched "the compartments in the machine and looked diligently into grips and handbags" for alcohol. The *Herald* wrote that because the dentist "does not drink intoxicants, he was particularly wroth and felt greatly outraged. He feared that his dentist friends might think he is known to the officers of the law and that they habitually search his car for intoxicants."[1] The article noted that others had the same experience and warned that thousands of indignant tourists could be driven away by these heavy-handed tactics. When James Allison, Fisher's friend, ally, and a prominent businessman, was fined after liquor was found secretly hidden in his aquarium in Miami Beach, Fisher wrote to Allison that the *Herald* had treated the matter very decently. Clearly, both newspapers used their power to sway opinion on the Prohibition issue. Marjory Stoneman Douglas, columnist for the *Herald*, wrote on August 17, 1920 that "It is a wise man who knows his own home brew."

Unlike Dean, Fisher admired Henry Flagler. In 1920, Fisher started building the Flagler Memorial on a 3-acre island (now Monument Island) in Miami Beach, near Fisher's under-construction Flamingo Hotel. The monument was to be 100

The Flagler Memorial was built by Carl Fisher in 1920, between the Flamingo Hotel and Star Island, in honor of Henry Flagler.

The Art Center, on the west side of Liberty Avenue between Twenty-third Street and the Collins Canal, was owned and operated by Mrs. C.G. Wheeler-Jones and provided Miami Beach with some of its first organized cultural and literary activities.

feet and 6 inches tall, and to have 4 sides that represented engineering, labor, education, and agriculture.

Despite the Fisher-Dean differences over Prohibition and railroad influence, the *Metropolis*, as well as the *Herald*, had special news sections on different parts of the county in 1920, and both gave significant and nearly always positive coverage to Miami Beach. The *Miami Herald* had sections that at different times were called "Miami Beach News," "News of Miami Beach," "Miami Beach," and "Personals." The *Miami Metropolis* had sections that were variously called "Beach Brevities" (very short listings), "Beach Personals," "Miami Beach News," and "Beach Notes." The *Miami Metropolis*, the *Weekly Miami Metropolis*, and the *Miami Daily Metropolis* were all published by Dean, and generally carried the same information. On December 1, Line Harger of the city's publicity department reported that the *Miami Metropolis* had established a news bureau at the Alton Beach Realty Company's office, Fisher's company.

In December 1920, when there was a small drive to change the name of Miami Beach to "Miami-by-the-Sea," the *Miami Metropolis* changed the name of its section on Miami Beach to "Miami Beach by the Sea." The city's name was not changed, and the city established its first post office with the name of Miami Beach that same month. The *Metropolis* described Miami Beach as the "Social Center of the Florida Peninsula in the Very Heart of America's Greatest Playground" and "Where the Atlantic Surfs to the Shore and Zephyrs are Laden With Constant Delights." Both newspapers apparently published verbatim (as "objective" news) items that were sent in by individuals and vested interests.

During the winter, most attention was given to the social life and sports life of winter residents or tourists, but in the off-season, most attention was given to local people and events. The two newspapers, each with a community section, left a rich research source of Miami Beach life in 1920.

In November 1920, Mrs. C.G. Wheeler-Jones, at the Art Center, began publication of her society journal for Miami Beach, the *Jackdaw*. Marjory Stoneman Douglas, who later became famous for writing *The Everglades: River of Grass* (1947) and died in 1998 at the age of 103, was one of the writers. On Sunday, December 19, the first issue of the *Jackdaw* came out. With 12 pages, the little "but sparkling" journal was said to be "bubbling over with interesting comment, much of which is between the lines, and all of which pertains to beach folks and their friends and passions."

Described as being for "the gossip-loving public's edification and delight," the journal was the result of editor Arnold L. Hart's literary ability. It was advertised as a publication that "knows all about you and tells it too, sometimes." It certainly was not a competitor to the two major newspapers, but it was at all newsstands and presented a unique perspective of Miami Beach. Reflecting Miami Beach's diversity in origins, Hart was 34 years old, single, and from England. By 1922, he would be a reporter for the *Miami Herald* and living at the Green Tree Inn in Miami.

Miami Beach also did not yet have an acting theater in 1920, necessitating more trips to Miami for theatergoers. Val C. Cleary, future mayor of Miami Beach (1930–1932 and 1941–1943), who was in real estate but who also described himself in the 1920 census as a theatrical actor, had the title role in *What Happened to Jones* in Miami in November. His wife, Grace (Pickert) Cleary, who described herself as a theatrical actress in the census, also was in the play. Grace came from an acting family. Her parents, two sisters, and a brother-in-law all described themselves as being in the theater. All of the family, including Val and Grace, lived together in one residence in Miami Beach in 1920. Early in 1921, Cleary would play the leading juvenile role in *Call of the Heart*, which was the closing bill for the Pickert Company at the Park Theater in Miami. On March 3, 1923, in a column in the *Herald*, Marjory Stoneman Douglas noted that the Miami area still had little background in music, art, and poetry, but that creative forces would emerge as the area developed an identity.

Miami Beach got its first telephone exchange in June 1919, a manual switchboard in the operator's residence on Second Street between Collins Avenue and Ocean Drive. Nevertheless, the rapid growth in demand could not be met. In Miami, the situation was much worse. In January alone, 200 applications for telephones had been turned down, with little hope of receiving service until September. In March, a new telephone book for Miami included about 4,000 listings, whereas the book for August 1919 had about 3,000 listings.

Meanwhile, the South Atlantic Telephone and Telegraph Company had been trying to get a 30-year franchise for Miami Beach, but strong opposition had developed to a proposed 10¢ toll charge. In late February 1920, South Atlantic had a new proposal that called for an automatic system instead of enlarging and improving the present system. Fisher supported the new telephone system proposal and, on March 17, the city council approved the proposal with a third reading. The vote was six to one, with only council president Norton voting against the proposal, which still required approval by Miami Beach voters. It was expected that the telephone company would not be able to have automatic equipment installed by the end of the year because of a backlog with manufacturers, but it planned to put a cable across the causeway, build a new outside plant, and erect a new building at Miami Beach.

On May 12, 1920, a headline article announced that a telephone building, to house the telephone exchange and living quarters for the company employees, would be built on the west side of Meridian Avenue, three lots south of Eleventh Street. Miami Beach now had less than 100 telephones and the new automatic system would be able to handle 1,400. The new Flamingo Hotel, scheduled to open in January, planned to install telephones in each room, a total of 200 automatic telephones. The Lincoln Hotel also ordered a private exchange with 60 automatic telephones. The general manager of the telephone company was optimistic, expecting the automatic system to be ready by November 1, 1920. Miami Beach was getting an automatic system before Miami because it was smaller and the necessary amount of equipment could be obtained more easily. Meanwhile, the public vote on the franchise was set for three months in the future, August 14, 1920.

Shortly before the election, the telephone company installed a special wire directly to the new fire headquarters in the city hall building in the 600-block of Collins Avenue. Although in many cities tubular steel poles were replacing wooden ones, the local company used the latter and expressed some regret that the unsightly poles would disfigure an attractive boulevard. The installing of the automatic system took place mostly in September and October. Meanwhile, in Miami, recognizing that the automatic systems would not be available until the summer of 1921, the telephone company installed switchboards that were purchased from closing military camps and hired 9 more operators, for a total of 30, at the same time. Miami Beach was indeed lucky in obtaining telephones. New York, Detroit, Chicago, Atlanta, and other large cities were waiting for such systems.

The local newspapers reported on October 22, 1920 that the telephone company had applied to the Florida Railroad Commission for a rate increase in Miami Beach and, the next day, 300 telephones for the Miami Beach automatic system had arrived. Miami Beach was close to doing away with the "old tinny small-village" type where a crank was turned to get an operator. The company manager said they were going from "the ridiculous to the sublime." Meanwhile, the city council had appointed a committee to look into the new rates request.

By the middle of December, the papers informed Miami Beach readers that the automatic telephone would be a Christmas gift to Miami Beach, scheduled to be ready by December 22. A pole line also was being built on the alley in order to

This 1921 photo shows Miami Beach policeman L.A. Jones (left) and another police officer using one of Miami Beach's new telephones.

take the telephone wires off of Collins Avenue. December 22 came and went, Christmas came and went, and, on December 26, a local journalist reported that the new system would be in operation in a few days. A new telephone directory was being delivered on December 27 and 28, to be effective after December 28. The total number of telephone subscribers was 80, consisting of 39 residences, 37 businesses, city hall, the fire department, the United States Coast Guard Station, and the United States Radio Station. Growth was so great, however, that any telephone book was soon outdated. Another directory was scheduled for February 1, 1921 and would be part of the Miami directory.

The telephone company recognized that the new system might be a little complicated at first and informed readers that a representative would come to their homes if necessary to give instructions on how to operate the new automated telephone system. An article informed readers that Miami Beach subscribers could call each other without an operator, but that they had to dial "0" and give their call to an operator to reach Miami.

The toll charge between Miami Beach and Miami was 10¢. No operators worked at the Miami Beach office and all business records were held at the Miami office. On December 27, 1920, the newspapers reported that the system doubtless would be completed on December 29. On the previous day, the telephone company placed a large advertisement in the *Miami Metropolis* stating that the system would be in operation on December 30. Would Miami Beach get automatic telephones in 1920? The problem was in making connection with the cross-bay section. In the meantime, the telephone company had been devoting at least a half-hour giving instructions in each home that had requested help. The directory still was not delivered, but was promised within a few days. Miami Beach did obtain its first automatic telephone system on December 30, 1920.

Telegrams remained a major method of communication in 1920 and the Miami Beach branch of the Western Union Telegraph Company opened on the first day of the year, "ideally located" at the Ocean Side Inn. Day and night telegrams, cables, and wireless messages were possible because of a complete installation. Construction soon started on Western Union's concrete terminal station/cable relay house on the northwest corner of Fifth Street and Meridian Avenue. All cables operated by the Western Union Telegraph Company to the Bahamas and countries to the south of the United States were being diverted from Galveston, New Orleans, and other cities to Miami, thus making Miami, or Miami Beach, the greatest cable center in the United States. In early July, Western Union planned to begin laying the cable for the South American cable system and a cable ship from a northern port was expected off Miami Beach to begin laying the cable from Miami Beach to Cuba.

A controversy had developed over the laying of the cable between Miami and Barbados within the 3-mile limit of the United States. The federal government

The New Automatic Telephone System
At Miami Beach

We have at great expense and effort provided an entirely new telephone system for Miami Beach, which will compare favorably with any system of its size in the United States. This splendid new system will be placed in service on Thursday, December 30th.

EACH SUBSCRIBER WILL RECEIVE INDIVIDUAL NOTICE WHEN TO BEGIN USING HIS NEW TELEPHONE

The telephones to be placed in service Thursday will be principally those subscribers who have had service under the old system. New orders now on file with us will be handled promptly after January 1st. The majority of telephones at the beach under the new system will be private lines, and no more than two parties will be connected on the same line under any condition.

It has been necessary to change many numbers at Miami Beach, and a special directory will be delivered to the beach subscribers before the new system is placed in service. Another directory will be issued on or about February 15th, 1921.

Special attention is directed to the fact that the quickest service will be obtained on calls between Miami and Miami Beach, if the call is placed by number instead of specifying some particular person. If the call is placed by number it will, in most cases, be completed immediately. If a particular person is called for, the service will necessarily be slower.

Each Miami Beach subscriber will be supplied with a pamphlet containing full instructions as to the use of the new system, and is requested to study this pamphlet carefully. If the use of the new system is not clear after reading pamphlet, upon request, a representative of the company will call and render further assistance.

All persons at Miami Beach desiring telephone service who have not placed an order for it are requested to call at our Miami office at once and file application.

SOUTH ATLANTIC TELEPHONE and TELEGRAPH COMPANY

FRANK B. SHUTTS,
President

F. W. WEBSTER,
Gen. Mgr.

The New Automatic Telephone System at Miami Beach gave detailed instructions. (Miami Herald.)

was concerned that England would have control of the cables from Barbados, and had issued a general order stopping all cable construction across the local channels. The United States government ordered vessels to Miami to prevent the laying of telegraph cables. "Southern City Blockaded 1st Time Since 1861" was the headline in the *Miami Herald* on August 11. "Happily, however, it is no crisis brought about by an uncompromising demand for the integrity of state rights, but to prevent a cable ship entering the port of Miami, the most southerly city on the Florida mainland."[2]

Five Western Union men who had been in Miami Beach since mid-September, waiting for the South American cable to be laid, were recalled to New York in mid-November. The men had been living in a cottage on Commerce Street that the company had rented for them, but the presence of "so many" men had led to constant surveillance. They had expected to go to Havana to work on the cable there.

On the night of November 26, eight armed men from two submarines were on guard duty throughout the night near Fifth Street, ostensibly to prevent the Western Union cable-laying gang from trying to drop the connecting section of the Barbados cable. Western Union officials said the company had no plans to lay the cable until the matter was straightened out, and that the show of armed strength by the Navy was moving picture stuff. The *Miami Daily Metropolis* reported that the subchaser was drawn up tight against the tiny and inoffensive-looking little Western Union barge, which was about 12 feet by 16 feet.

On December 1, 1920, the Western Union Telegraph Company announced that it had definitely decided to remove all its cable operations from Miami Beach and establish its international cable base at Havana. The *Miami Herald* noted that this announcement suddenly made Miami businessmen realize that this move would cost the city many hundreds of company employees and $1 million a year in business. An emergency meeting was called for representatives of many influential organizations to discuss the situation. Some local community leaders believed the government might not be altogether wrong in its position, but that if it was decided that the government was wrong, then the city should contact its senators and representatives. The year ended with Miami Beach's role in the telegraph business in doubt.

Miami Beach's beauty and growth attracted the attention of filmmakers across the country. In the last week of March, the Selznick Pictures Corporation was in Miami Beach shooting scenes for a movie, *The Flapper*. Olive Thomas, one of the stars and "the world's most beautiful girl," was a center of attraction, and people enjoyed the novelty of having their pictures taken, apparently with actors and actresses. In April, the Selznick production team shot several scenes at the Snowden home on Collins Avenue. The movie actors, actresses, and crews stayed at the Breakers Hotel.

On Saturday, December 18, Selznick Pictures Corporation was at the Miami Beach Baths to begin shooting some scenes for *The Gilded Lies*. Members of the company, including Martha Mansfield, formerly of the Ziegfield Follies and celebrated as "America's Prettiest magazine cover girl," had arrived the day before. Eugene O'Brien, "a movie star of the first magnitude," who was remembered as "The Perfect Lover," would arrive on Monday. William P.S. Earle, the noted director, said that *The Woman Game* had caused other directors to notice Miami Beach and that the officials of the Selznick corporation were so impressed by the settings of *The Flapper* that they immediately made plans to locate more pictures in Miami and Miami Beach. He stated that principal scenes of two pictures, *Gilded Payment* and *Received Payment*, would be made at Miami. He said that some people had not had a chance to see *The Woman Game*, which starred Elaine Hammerstein, so he was going to arrange to have it shown in Miami again. He expected to film scenes at Miami Beach, the Deering Estate, and other beauty spots of Florida during the next week. The *Miami Metropolis* reported that Miami and the area's beaches and waters would be shown in more than 6,000 theaters in the spring, and that Miami and Miami Beach would be given credit as the locations.

All of the excitement in Miami Beach led to the desire to capture it in moving pictures and photographs. Earle Emlay, inventor of a new stereospeed camera, was in Miami Beach at the invitation of Fisher. On January 20, 1920, he lined up all the children playing on the sands and those staying at the Breakers Hotel to make animated pictures, trying to get them "to smile, laugh, cry, or look dignified." The next day, he took pictures of the Miami Beach Golf links, of the players and the surroundings. On March 14, the Miami Beach Baths staged a swimming meet, with the most remarkable stunt being the underwater swimming of Buck Silas, and Emlay was there to snap the swimmers for the movies. Emlay made moving pictures of golf, dining, and lawn tennis matches at Miami Beach, and showed pictures at the Hippodrome Theater in Miami, where they were a popular feature. By April, Emlay and an assistant were preparing for six weeks of photographing Miami Beach from the sky, describing them as short movies that would show why the area was so aptly called "The Playground of America." Emlay's moving pictures had made a great sensation in New York and, as with other new inventions or improvements, the people in Miami Beach were excited by the new fast-moving camera and wanted to see themselves in moving pictures.

Photography also was a great attraction in Miami Beach in 1920. Claude Matlack, a locally famous photographer, who had exclusive rights to make pictures at the Miami Beach Casino and on the polo grounds, opened his casino photographic studio at night to invite dancers to be photographed while in their evening dresses. He had a store in Miami, but he also built a studio in Miami Beach and made hundreds of local shots with diverse settings. Some of Matlack's photographs have been destroyed, but thousands of his photographs remain in good condition. Many of the photographs in this book were taken by Matlack. The people of Miami Beach in 1920 were excited by photographs, as well as by moving pictures, and Miami Beach today owes a great debt to Matlack and the people for their part in preserving the city's heritage for later generations to enjoy. Their 1920 excitement helped to preserve the history of the making of America's greatest winter resort.

5. Hotels, Inns, Apartment Houses, and Restaurants

Miami Beach's first hotel was the Atlantic Beach Hotel, built in 1915 on the northwest corner of Ocean Drive and First Street by William J. Brown. It later became known simply as Brown's Hotel. Brown had been born in Glasgow, Scotland in 1879, came to New York at age 15, and moved to Miami in 1904. Brown also was a successful plumber and his wife, Margaret Johnson Brown, a native of Belfast, Ireland, helped run the hotel. Brown's Hotel was a two-story building, with a series of kitchens on the concrete first floor and bedrooms on the second floor. Built completely of Dade County pine, Brown's Hotel is one of the few 1920 buildings remaining in Miami Beach.

Perhaps the guests at Brown's in 1920 talked about the story that had surfaced the previous summer about a buried ship. On June 9, 1919, the *Miami Metropolis* had reported William J. Brown's story that in 1915, when he began excavating to build the hotel's foundation, he had found the hull of an ancient 130-foot-long ship buried 2 feet under the sand. Workers had dug down to the deck, found no treasure, and simply filled back in the sand and built on top of the ship. In 1998, new owners of the building did not find the ship and, in early 2002, when the hotel was jacked up and moved back so that a replica of the original front porch could be built between the hotel and the sidewalk, no ship was found.

In early 1920, there were several newsworthy pieces, carried by the local papers, featuring the guests and life at Brown's Hotel. At the end of April 1920, E. Cecil Canova of Miami, his wife, and their four little daughters were staying at Brown's for two months, which the local papers detailed. Canova was to assist the county tax assessor, who was soon to begin assessing Miami Beach properties. Although it was almost May, Brown's Hotel was still getting northern visitors. Brown's had its own social life and when several guests left for Chicago in early May, Brown's gave a "rather notable" farewell, a marshmallow roast and large bonfire that lit up all the south part of the beach for hours. However, a few weeks later, when guests at Brown's planned to have another bonfire to observe a birthday, a high wind prevented it. The celebrants had to settle for a supper and special electric decorations of the pergola and the beach walk.

Miami Beach's first hotel, known for most of its life as Brown's Hotel, was built in 1915 and is undergoing historical renovation as this book goes to press.

The Lincoln Hotel, owned by Carl Fisher and Miami Beach's most prestigious hotel as 1920 started, had been built on the south side of Lincoln Road between Miami (Washington) Avenue and Drexel Avenue (nearer to Drexel) in 1916. Originally an apartment building, it was changed to have some hotel rooms even before it opened on January 20, 1917. A major addition was added to the east in 1920, taking the building all the way from Drexel Avenue to Miami (Washington) Avenue. The hotel had been designed by the locally famous architect August "Gus" Geiger, who designed a number of buildings in the area. In 1920, the Lincoln Hotel, about two blocks from the Atlantic Ocean, advertised itself as being located in the center of all the beach attractions. The hotel was still listed in the 1920 city directory as the Lincoln Apartment Hotel, but usually was referred to as simply the Lincoln Hotel.

The hotel was a big success, needed more rooms, and was undergoing extensive additions as 1920 began. Workers were rushing work on the second-story walls, but the addition would not be finished for the season even though there already were enough requests to fill it. When the Lincoln opened on January 20, the winter season was in full bloom, and the hotel was already turning people away. By early March, the Lincoln's 35 new rooms were already booked for the 1921 season.

On April 6, the Lincoln Hotel closed for the spring and summer after enjoying its most successful winter season in history. Like all other hotels and apartments at the beach, the Lincoln Hotel had enjoyed overflow crowds from early in the season to practically the closing day. The new addition, which would more than double the capacity, was almost completed and expected to be finished during the summer, ready for an early opening in the fall.

The Breakers Hotel also had been an apartment building, but was converted into a hotel by Mrs. Tatum Wofford. It opened for the 1917–1918 winter season. In 1920, the Breakers, located at 2422 Collins Avenue, still advertised itself as the only hotel on the oceanfront in Miami Beach and as the only hotel in Florida within 100 feet of the ocean. Mrs. Tatum Wofford, that is, Mrs. Ora Bucks Wofford, a native of Georgia, like her husband, was described as a popular hostess in Miami Beach. She would later build the Wofford Hotel at 2400 Collins Avenue, just south of the Breakers Hotel.

The Breakers was a popular place for private parties for luncheon and dinner, and "La Terrace" was added in late January for "the smart set." The opening was in the form of a tea dansant, with a specially selected string quartet. The Aero Limited had planes that landed in front of the Breakers Hotel and many of its guests enjoyed taking these plane rides. Social occasions at the hotel frequently made the news. By early February, every room was filled and the hotel was booked through the season. Many important guests at the Breakers were named and identified in the local papers. Mrs. Wofford announced that the hotel was enjoying a record season.

The same day that the Lincoln Hotel's closing was announced, the Breakers Hotel received a small news item when two of its guests, who were returning from Havana, landed in front of the Breakers Hotel in an Aero Limited plane after

This August 28, 1920 photo shows the original Lincoln Hotel on the right and the 1920 addition on the left. Across Lincoln Road to the north is the golf course. Until enlargement and improvement, a small dirt road was between the hotel and the golf course.

only a five-hour flight from Havana, leaving Havana at 1:30 and landing at the Breakers at 6:30. Such flights were still novel enough to rate special mention in the newspapers. The Breakers continued to have newspaper notices about hotel and luncheon guests.

The Lincoln Hotel, the Breakers Hotel, and Brown's Hotel remained the most popular hotels for 1920, and their overloaded success certainly proved the need for more hotels. As 1920 began, Fisher had stated that Miami Beach needed a dozen more hotels of 60 rooms each as soon as they could be built, and announced that his Alton Beach Realty Company would give special inducements to investors through sales of sites and through taking stock in any meritorious company. Fisher started building the Flamingo Hotel in early 1920 on Biscayne Bay (he avoided the ocean), with a planned opening date of December 1, 1920. However, the Flamingo would not open until December 31, 1920 and the need for more hotel rooms would still exist.

Because of the tremendous demand for skilled labor and mechanics for building the Flamingo Hotel and other projects during 1920, plus the added expense of transporting workers from Miami, Fisher also began building an 80-room hotel to house 300 workers. The hotel was being built on the north side of Canal Road (now Dade Boulevard) at the high bridge. Although the structure was delayed because of a shortage of building material, it was expected to be finished by mid-June. Another building on the Allison, or old shipyard, site at the lower end of the beach already housed 150 men, but it was also being used for loading supplies. Despite these plans, most of the construction workers assembled at the corner of Waddell Street and Avenue C in Miami at 7 a.m. and were conveyed to Miami Beach by large motor trucks.

With winter guests gone, except for a small number of tourists who stayed and many daily visitors from the Miami mainland, life in Miami Beach was basically the quiet, small-town type. With less attention being given to bigger establishments during the summer, some of the small inns received more publicity in the local papers. The Ocean Side Inn on the north side of Twenty-third Street between Collins Avenue and Liberty Avenue did not receive much publicity, but it did receive publicity when the Miami Beach branch of the Western Union Telegraph Company opened its headquarters there on January 1, 1920. On February 25, 1920, the inn received more publicity when it hosted Lieutenant Commander Alexander Procofieff-Seversky, a Russian ace, and his mother. Staying for several weeks, the "not yet 25 years of age" hero of World War I and winner of the St. George's Cross was described by local journalists as one of the most distinguished visitors in Miami Beach. By the end of April, like others in the booming little city, H.V. Duval, proprietor of the Ocean Side Inn, was making extensive changes. The exterior was being tinted in pink, matching the casino. The inn was scheduled to reopen on June 1, 1920 to cater to Miami people during the summer, serving special Sunday dinners.

The Bridge Inn, on the northwest corner of Dade Boulevard and West Avenue, also did not receive much publicity, but after the Lincoln Hotel closed at the end

An aerial shot of the Breakers Hotel shows the ocean to the left (east), and Collins Avenue and Pancoast Lake to the right (west). The house in the rectangular area between the ocean and Collins Avenue is the John S. Collins home.

of the winter season, many of its guests moved to the Bridge Inn. The inn was full of tourists who found April, May, and even June delightful at the beach. John L. Berry, in charge of construction at the Flamingo Hotel, bought the inn. Carrie, his wife, prepared excellent food and the inn was considered "the place" for home cooking. Carrie Berry was a popular hostess and managed the inn with great success, having an average of 70 people at the dinner tables. John Berry planned to remodel the dormitory and increase its capacity by 50 people. Later in the year, the Bridge Inn would be overflowing as many of the department heads connected with the building of the Flamingo Hotel made it their headquarters.

The small Beach Inn was one of the establishments on the northeast corner of the intersection of Ocean Drive and Biscayne Avenue (South Pointe Drive) between Hardie's Casino and Smith's Casino. The inn received brief newspaper mentions as having guests. Mrs. J.E. (Ida) Reynolds, proprietor of the hotel, even made the front page of the *Miami Daily Metropolis* on April 17, 1920 when a squall at the height of a storm the previous night blew her car off the causeway and into 4 feet of water upside down. She was not injured and, shortly after the accident, Dr. Carl H. Van Dyke of Miami Beach "came along in his machine and took her home."

While most attention in 1920 was given to hotels and some attention was given to inns, apartment houses also were doing a good business, helping fill the city's drastic need for housing and occasionally receiving publicity. On January 24,

1920, Theodore Schmitt, proprietor of the Toledo Apartments at 32 Collins Avenue, arrived for the winter, his first visit since he had been injured by an exploding kerosene can two years earlier. In early April, after another successful season in which people had been turned away daily by the dozens, Schmitt started adding 18 more apartments, bringing the total to 44 apartments and making the Toledo the largest apartment house in Miami Beach. And, in late May, Schmitt cashed a mysterious draft for $500, which he had received from New York. After failing to trace the mysterious draft, Schmitt concluded that someone was sending the money as "conscience money" for some wrong deed done in the past.

The 11-unit Olive Apartments could be found at 126 Ocean Drive and was refurnished and equipped with electric stoves during 1920. Charles LeJeune, one of the wealthy grove owners of the Coconut Grove section, who had spent much of the previous three or four years at Miami Beach, returned to the beach in April 1920 for an indefinite stay, and took a suite at the Olive Apartments. In June, Isabelle Krome of Homestead, the wife of William J. Krome, the noted engineer who finished the FEC Railroad's overseas extension to Key West, and her family were also staying at the Olive Apartments. The apartments received another famous resident in July, "Smith of the Olive Apartments," who was a "raw foodist" and never ate cooked food of any kind, including vegetables, and lived principally on fruits, olive oil, and nuts. The Olive Apartments had been built in

This is a May 2002 view of the east side of Hale's Apartments, one of the few buildings left from 1920. The front entrance is on Commerce Street on the right of the photograph. In the background to the left is the 38-floor Murano at Portofino, and to the right is the 33-story Yacht Club at Portofino.

1914 as a wheelchair house. This had failed and John F. Olive had purchased the building, first using it as a club and then as an apartment house. Olive served on the Miami Beach Council from October 28, 1918 to December 12, 1919.

The Pratt Apartments were located at 20 Collins Avenue between Biscayne Avenue (South Pointe Drive) and First Street. One of the largest apartment houses in Miami Beach, the Pratt Apartments was three stories high and had 21 apartments. The Pratt was sold in March for $35,000 with a full house. The new owners soon changed the name to the Hibiscus Apartments.

The Hale Apartments were located at 850 Commerce Street, west of Miami (Washington) Avenue and a little east of Jefferson Avenue. The apartments were managed by Mabel Hale, who split her time between Miami Beach and Brooklyn, New York and who, in 1946, sold them to Abraham Wiener. This apartment building is one of the few 1920 buildings still standing in Miami Beach. The Grove Apartments, at 209 Biscayne Avenue, were described in June as "new." Around September, Carl Fisher bought the 8-unit El Mar Apartments, just west of Collins Avenue, on the south side of Twenty-first Street, as housing for his workers because of an apartment shortage. The Dade Apartments, a new 19-unit apartment building with two rooms per apartment, opened on the northeast corner of Alton Road and Dade Boulevard late in December.

Although the tourist season had almost ended by mid-March and visitors were "getting away as fast as they can," all apartment houses in Miami Beach were still fairly full and people were still making reservations for April. Many of these visitors were people who had been unable to secure rooms or apartments earlier because of the overflow, but were determined to spend a few weeks by the ocean before returning north. Because of the booming season in Miami Beach, there was a demand for even more apartment houses.

With most of the tourists gone, the local newspapers started emphasizing local residents with reports on who was going where, who was visiting whom, etc. These notices illustrated the great extent to which local people became tourists themselves during the summer. Many people spent much of the summer at resorts, both in the mountains and at the seashore. Asheville and other small towns in the North Carolina mountains, like Brevard, were quite popular. Many of the local residents also visited relatives and friends in their former hometowns and, today, these reports give examples of the great variety of background among Miami Beach residents in 1920.

Mr. and Mrs. Frank O. Van Deren departed for Indianapolis for five months; Mayor and Mrs. Thomas J. Pancoast attended the national Rotary Club convention in Atlantic City, New Jersey and visited family in that state; Mr. and Mrs. W.E. Brown joined the pilgrimage of Shriners to Portland, Oregon; City Council president and Mrs. W.E. Norton left for Hot Springs, Arkansas (they had not been away since before the beginning of the war); and the Witcher family left to spend the entire summer in the Adirondacks before returning to Miami Beach in the late fall. Captain (and city councilman) Charles R. Meloy went to visit his former hometown of New Haven, Connecticut and other places. One of the people who remembered Charlie Meloy visiting New Haven was Olin Meloy, Charlie's then-14-year-old nephew, who in November 1997 at the age of 91, recalled that after moving south, Charlie Meloy had used boats to carry cypress logs from a swamp, and that later he had three boats for fishing: the *Savalo*, the *Stanger*, and the *Dorothy*. After Charlie Meloy returned to Miami Beach, Edith Meloy planned to leave for New York to visit relatives. Captain John H. Welch, who was not an official resident of Miami Beach in 1920 but was credited with building a house on Miami Beach in 1913 and for seconding the motion to incorporate Miami Beach in 1915, left for Tampa and then the mountains of North Carolina for a month.

The local newspapers named about 350 people who left town for parts of the summer, with many references to "and family" without names of all family members. Among the named individuals, about 100 were in the North Carolina mountains, but over 20 states and other locations (including Canada, Cuba, and Switzerland) were listed as being former homes or the homes of relatives. The local newspapers also noted that many returning residents were reporting that the weather in the Miami area was preferable to that experienced elsewhere. Even some of those who liked North Carolina were glad to get home.

The stress of the "rat race" in a hectic environment was implied occasionally when a local journalist would comment that a Miami Beach resident had to get out of town for rest and recuperation. In early June 1920, the Harry S. Bastian family was planning a trip north to last several months, with the notation that Bastian was making the trip for rest and recuperation from construction work. Dan Hardie returned to Miami Beach in November after five months out of town, including four months in Manitou, Colorado for resting advised by his physician. Other items in the papers mentioned people leaving town for a rest because the men were overworked by Miami Beach's hectic growth.

The notices also reported some of the summer activities in the city. Oliver P. Searing of the Miami Beach water department announced that 250 of the approximately 300 houses in the city had water service. Ida Reynolds, wife of John E. Reynolds, sold her lease of the Beach Inn. Miami Beach municipal judge John L. Crist and his wife moved into their new home at 811 Collins Avenue. Judge Armstead Brown of Miami (who was listed in the Miami Beach census) was having his cottage on Collins Avenue readied for occupancy. In 1925, Judge Brown moved to Tallahassee, where he, from 1925 to 1946, was a justice of the Supreme Court of Florida, including about three years as chief justice.

Attention was also given to businesses that remained open during the summer. For guests who stayed in Miami Beach during the summer, Brown's Hotel remained open and popular. Bonfires were still popular and, on June 15, 1920, there was an evening of entertainment that, with the finest illumination of the beach so far during the summer, lasted for two hours and attracted many people from all parts of the city. People sat in chairs facing the ocean, supper was served at tables, and a phonograph provided music. Then, the people walked over to Smith's Casino for night bathing and a swimming exhibition. Around June,

Alwilda Stanton, wife of William J. Stanton, had opened the Stanton Refreshment Depot at the corner of Biscayne Avenue (South Pointe Drive) and Ocean Drive, as well as a first-class cafeteria, specializing in homemade foods, in the Inlet Goodie Shop in the Lummus building. As June came to an end and the summer continued, there were a number of other "Beach Brevities" dealing with the small things of daily life, noting, for example, that J.B. Russell had made a trip to Miami the previous week, that Jerry Pinder had gone to Rock Harbor down among the Keys to visit a sister, and that Carl Fisher was scheduled to arrive at his offices on Friday. There were a lot of local tourists from Miami at the beaches during the summer, but for people who lived in Miami Beach all year, it was a slower life before the hectic winter season began again.

With G.A. Gloor as proprietor and Joe Weiss as manager, the Sunshine Inn at Smith's Casino was the scene of a banquet on July 20 for 20 men from the W.A. Riddle truck and tractor distributorship in Miami. Activities included the pool, jumping the breakers, a rub-down, an excellent banquet served by Joe Weiss, smokers, and post-prandial (after dinner) exercises. The Seaside Cafe also made news when it was noted that Pearl Parker, who had bought the cafe earlier in the

This is a May 2002 view of the north side of Brown's Hotel. On the left side of the photograph is Ocean Drive. In the background to the left, close to where Smith's Casino was located, is the 40-story Continuum under construction. In the middle is the 25-story South Pointe Tower, the first of the high-rises, built in 1987, and to the right is the 42-story Portofino Towers. Across the street from Portofino Towers is Joe's, and a half block west of Joe's is the Hale Apartments.

The Breakers Hotel is shown from the south side. Carl Fisher preferred the bay for his luxury hotels, but the Breakers was proud of being Miami Beach's only hotel on the ocean.

summer, had not had her expectations met and, thus, had sold the cafe to Anna McKay. Hardie's Casino hosted the Woman's Aid Society of the Presbyterian Church in Miami for an all-day meeting on July 23. The women went bathing and had a picnic lunch at noon.

With the slowness of summer, and despite the season's threatening clouds and occasional showers, a group of young people from Miami enjoyed a straw ride to Miami Beach for bathing and a picnic luncheon at Hardie's Casino, followed by a ride up to Fulford Beach, now close to Sunny Isles. A short distance away, Brown's Hotel was hosting another of its popular moonlight bathing parties and massive bonfires. On August 27, Brown's was the scene of a birthday party for a little girl and more than 30 people were entertained by a watermelon party illuminated by Brown's affinity for ever-popular bonfires.

Some Miami people lived in Miami Beach during the summer for several months. In August, Brown's Hotel gave a farewell party for Jack and Martha Yarborough, who were moving to their new home in Miami after being at Brown's for three months, and supper was served at a new pavilion on the beach. Soon afterwards, DeLeon's Restaurant on Ocean Drive hosted a dinner for Rear Admirals Decker and Anderson of the United States Navy. Leon DeLeon, the owner and "noted chef," and the only Italy-born resident in the 1920 census, served an Italian dinner that won the admirals' praise.

While the Breakers Hotel was closed to hotel guests during the summer, in the summer of 1920, for the second year, it operated as a YWCA summer camp, which opened on August 10 for a ten-week session. The camp's goal was to provide a pleasant vacation on the seashore at the lowest possible cost, particularly for businesswomen. Other women were welcome if there were vacancies, but they paid $15 per week for room and board, while employed women paid $10. Visitors were usually received on Thursday and Sunday afternoons. The camp continued to be popular and girls aged 10 to 18 enjoyed parties. The simple joys of weekly Friday afternoon swimming for girls was described in the society section of the *Miami Metropolis* on August 28, noting that shrieks of delight issued from the girls, who found the water a trifle chilly.

In early September, the Wigwam, a tent restaurant at the corner of Biscayne Avenue (South Pointe Drive) and Ocean Drive, was moved so that construction could begin on a four-story building. It soon reopened just north of Hardie's Casino where the lunchrooms were continuously filled by people who wouldn't leave the beach long enough for a regular meal at home or in a hotel. In December, Ludwig Mieses, proprietor of the Wigwam, recorded a 99-year lease for the property, agreeing to pay $3,500 a year for 99 years. The 99-year lease later became very popular in Miami Beach.

Shortly before Labor Day, the *Miami Daily Metropolis* notified readers that one-piece bathing suits would still be allowed, but wiener roasts, fish fries, marshmallow toasts, and early morning bacon bats were to be allowed only with a permit. A compromise was soon reached, so that people could still have fires as long as the fire was not more than 10 feet back from the high watermark. Shortly later, the Recreation Club held a Labor Day celebration, with a beach party, a wiener roast with a fire on the beach, and games around the fire.

The YWCA continued to hold Friday afternoon beach parties, announcing on September 30, 1920, that the last beach party for the season would be held the next day because "the opening of the Miami public schools Monday [October 4] make it necessary to discontinue them." Forty-four girls enjoyed the last party, with regrets that the parties had to be discontinued. The *Miami Herald* listed all the girls present. The "Y" Camp concluded its second summer session on October 12, 1920 after an enjoyable ten weeks of surf bathing, water sports, long hikes, evening bonfires, coconut hunts, auto rides, and Friday evening stunt shows. Throughout the severe heat of the summer, the camp had helped the women to go back to their offices with more vitality and more interest in their work.

Regardless of size, most businesses starting revving up for the winter season around October. In 1920, as in other years in that era, the summer season in Miami Beach was long, with county schools usually beginning in late September. In 1920, in Miami Beach, they did not begin until October 11 because of construction and hiring delays. Residents who had gone north had gradually returned to Miami Beach throughout the summer, but some did not return until early October.

As October arrived, more newspaper attention again began to be given to tourist spots in Miami Beach, although continued attention was given to the places that had remained open during the summer. Brown's Hotel served as a rescue area on October 28, 1920 when Mrs. W.A. Kell of Philadelphia, a guest at Brown's, almost drowned. Brown's Hotel sponsored a Halloween party for guests, former guests, and a number of beach residents. A special feature was a Scottish piper in full lamont plaids, kilts, and cap, with Scottish melodies and dances.

After being closed over the summer, the Lincoln Hotel reopened on November 5, 1920. The new addition, and expensive improvements on the old building, had been completed, although the furnishings for the addition were still being moved in. The addition included a 116-foot-long balcony and a large lobby to be used for entertainment. Ample fire escapes, continually lighted, and an abundant water supply were also included. Each of the new rooms had a large bathroom, and there were spacious halls, drawing rooms, and sitting rooms on each floor. The hotel now covered the entire block. The new addition was larger than the old part, but they were connected by the long dining room and a 126-foot-long loggia. The rooms at the back overlooked gardens, and the rooms on the front overlooked a golf course across a sandy-dirt street called Lincoln Road. The dining room had been enlarged to over 100 feet long by 60 feet wide, and the kitchen had been enlarged and equipped with the latest labor-saving devices.

Furnishings and decorations for the entire building had been done by Wanamaker's store in New York, and Fisher had spared no expense to make his establishment both comfortable and beautiful. The Lincoln Hotel would be supplied with milk, cream, and butter from its own dairy, Broad Ripple Farm, and vegetables would come from a farm in Miami Beach. Bernhard Lundberg, a native of Sweden, was the hotel's manager. Among the first guests were Carl G. Fisher; James A. Allison, president of the Miami Aquarium Association, who had just arrived on his auxiliary cruiser *L'Apache*; Dr. John Oliver LaGorce of *National Geographic Magazine*; and Thomas Shipp, a member of the advisory committee for the aquarium. Other early guests were Jane Fisher's parents, Mr. and Mrs. George Welch of Albany, New York, who were awaiting the completion of their six-room bungalow on James Avenue. James C. "Jimmy" Cooley, recently hired to manage Fisher's polo interests, arrived on December 1, 1920.

With the new addition, and the most expensive and comfortable furniture, the Lincoln Hotel was doing well. It had hosted many famous guests and was said to be a pleasant family hotel. The people working there said they were "not much" concerned about the Flamingo Hotel's imminent opening. The hotels aimed at different types of guests and both were owned by Carl Fisher. Lincoln guests included Charles E. Haggett and his wife. Mr. Haggett was known as the world's undefeated tennis player and was the new instructor for tennis in Miami Beach. United States Senator A.B. Cummins of Des Moines, Iowa was especially popular. Mrs. James A. Allison and her young daughter Cornelia, as well as Mrs. Allison's lovable but temperamental pet monkey Pat, were also staying at the Lincoln. In addition, the hotel had the distinction of housing one of the golf club's best women players, Mrs. F.R. Humpage, whose husband was a manager for Fisher's real estate.

The Lincoln Hotel might have been facing an impressive new competitor, the Flamingo Hotel, but there were two factors in its favor. First, as noted, Fisher

This postcard shows the expanded Lincoln Hotel and the Congregational Church on Lincoln Road. The church, now known as the Miami Beach Community Church, remains on bustling Lincoln Mall as one of the city's historic gems.

owned both of them and he was a very sharp businessman. The second factor was new and of tremendous importance. The big electric turbine of Fisher's Miami Beach Electric Company on the causeway was turned on for the first time on December 13, 1920 and, within a week or so, the company would be furnishing light and power to Miami Beach. Fisher had put the power plant on Causeway Terminal Island, a triangular section of filled land near the Miami Beach end of the causeway and the ship channel, so that it could be reached easily by either truck or barge.

After weeks of planning, on the night of December 21, 1920, after the electric plant opened, Lincoln Road blazed forth as a metropolitan way "when the 70 boulevard lights from the ocean to the bay [were] cut on for the first time." The lamps were 100 candlepower, nitrogen filled, with simple ornamented design, and a glass canopy. The lighting was planned to be brilliant compared to other streets and to emphasize the boulevard system. Lincoln Road was Fisher's dream street, his "Fifth Avenue of the South," modeled after the Rue de la Paix in Paris, which he had never seen. Fisher had designed it to be 100 feet wide with room for two sidewalks separated by buffers of decorative plantings. One sidewalk was to be for purposeful shoppers and the other for window shoppers and meanderers.

Lincoln Road had come a long way from its simple beginnings in 1905 when woodsmen, who were gathering mangrove bark for tannic acid, had cleared a wide path from the ocean to the bay. Fisher had built his own home at the east end of

Lincoln Road on the south side next to the Atlantic Ocean. Across the road, on the north side next to the Atlantic Ocean, was the palatial part-time home of F.A. Sieberling of Akron, Ohio, president of the Goodyear Tire and Rubber Company. This home, with a beautiful avenue of coconut palms along the shore to break the sea winds, had been purchased by Sieberling from John H. Hanan in early 1920. Just south of Fisher's home was the palatial home of Arthur C. Newby, who had been one of the original partners in the Miami Ocean View Company.

The Breakers Hotel opened in late November 1920 with new decorations and new kitchen equipment, and soon a large number of brilliantly striped lounge chairs and tables with gaily colored covers were put on the east front facing the ocean. The *Miami Herald* reported that "much favorable comment has been provoked by this added luxury for the convenience of the guests at the hotel." As the year ended, the Breakers Hotel reported that guests had been registering "thick and fast" during the last few weeks.

Brown's Hotel, as noted, remained open and busy throughout the year, and frequently had enjoyable activities for its guests. The guests also provided much of their own socialization. On Christmas night, there was a Christmas tree, presents, and storytelling. Rose Weiss did impersonations and Mrs. F. Martin gave a reading as part of the entertainment. The area around Brown's Hotel added to the joy of living there. Seventy years later, Rose Weiss's daughter Malvina remembered Miami Beach as being like a South Seas island, with a very natural life. Brown's was not luxurious like the Flamingo Hotel or the Lincoln Hotel, but it was a great life for people who lived in Miami Beach all year, for tourists who remained, and for Miami people who spent the summer at the beach.

This was the second Joe's Stone Crab Restaurant, probably in the 1940s. Shown on this postcard in the background is the original Joe's from 1920.

Rose Weiss had been at Brown's only a short time, having moved from New York because of asthma. On December 10, a brevity item in the *Miami Metropolis* noted that Weiss and her son Eugene of New York, and Sol Blanck of Brooklyn, were staying at Brown's Hotel, which had been redecorated and largely refurnished. The Rose and Jeremiah Weiss family would become Miami Beach's second permanent Jewish family, preceded only by the Joe and Jennie Weiss family (no relation) of Joe's Stone Crab fame. Rose Weiss, then 34 years old, would become very active in Miami Beach civic life, would design Miami Beach's flag, become referred to as the "Mama of South Beach," and live in Miami Beach 54 years until her death in 1974. In 1975, the Rose Weiss Park was dedicated in South Beach on the northeast corner of Washington Avenue and Second Street.

Like many resort areas in the United States, Miami Beach north of Fifth Street had restrictions against Jewish residents and guests, but in South Beach, established by the Lummus brothers from Georgia, there were no restrictions against Jews, although there were restrictions against African Americans. There, the Joe and Jennie Weiss family and the Rose and Jeremiah Weiss family would settle and make major contributions to Miami Beach. Rose Weiss was strongly devoted to her Jewish heritage, but she also was ecumenical in her community involvement as she participated in the Christmas program at Brown's Hotel. Despite restrictions, there were Jewish residents and hotel guests north of Fifth Street. Isidor Cohen, leader of the Miami Jewish community, was actively involved in real estate north of Fifth Street. For example, in 1920, Cohen was the agent when Nathan Goldman bought Dr. C.H. Van Dyke's house at 1428 Collins Avenue and when L. Shapiro bought (soon-to-be mayor) Thomas E. James's house at 1434 Collins Avenue. Indications are that, in 1927, for example, about a third of Miami Beach's Jewish residents lived north of Fifth Street.

Fisher had "selected" Jewish friends who met his social requirements, but he had restrictions against most Jews, as did much of the United States in that time period. An advertisement in early 1920, for example, to sell lots near the soon-to-open Causeway said that the lots were restricted. The Flamingo Hotel was viewed as especially anti-Semitic. Mehling writes that not only could Julius Fleischmann, Fisher's polo partner, not go to Fisher's clubhouse, but that United States circuit judge Julian W. Mack, who was also president of the Zionist Organization of America, president of the first American Jewish Congress, and first chairman of the Comité des Délégations Juives at the Versailles Peace Conference, was not allowed to stay at the Flamingo Hotel. Mehling continues, saying, "Until the late 1930s Jews were barred from almost all oceanfront hotels above Lincoln Road; it was not until World War II that a law banned display of restrictive signs such as 'No Jews or Dogs.' "[1]

While Jewish residents and visitors were unwelcome many places, African Americans received basically no welcome in Miami Beach in 1920 except as domestic workers and manual laborers. Black tourism workers had to carry an identification card, but as Howard Kleinberg has proven, helping correct a myth, white tourism workers were also required to carry the card. However, whites did not welcome African Americans and harassed them when they tried to bathe or swim in the ocean. This continued until the 1960s.[2] The *Miami Metropolis* illustrated the city's attitude toward blacks when it reported that on Sunday, January 2, 1921, "The arrival of negroes at south beach Sunday caused a little stir among the owners of places of amusement." There was no mention of unwelcome behavior, only an unwelcome presence.

Of course, in 1920, the inns and apartment houses had begun filling up as the winter season approached. The Ocean Side Inn, for example, had been thoroughly overhauled over the summer, with much new furniture and a French chef in charge of the kitchen. By November 13, the Toledo Apartments were rapidly being filled with season leases for the 1920–1921 winter season. A famous guest was Captain Arthur Sutton, who had the distinction of having been the first Allied officer to enter Berlin after the Armistice ended World War I in December 1918. Guests at the Grove Apartments were given a "House Warming" reception by the proprietors on December 2, 1920 with music, dancing, games, and refreshments. By early December, the Hale Apartments at 850 Commerce Street were filling up. The new Dade Apartments on the northeast corner of Alton Road and Dade Boulevard did not allow cooking, but the manager, Mrs. John Shoemaker, planned to open a cafe in a separate building in the rear of the apartments. Small newspaper items mentioned by individual name many guests who were arriving at the various apartment houses. The apartment houses did not get the attention that the major hotels did, but Miami Beach was still small enough that the newspapers could add some personal touch for apartment house guests.

Restaurants were also a part of the booming little city, especially during the winter, and small eating places were frequently opening and sometimes closing in the competitive market. A new eating house opened at the corner of Biscayne Avenue and Collins Avenue in mid-November. Mr. and Mrs. George Herman, who had a booth all summer near the Flamingo Hotel construction site for feeding workers, opened "a real Coney Island eating house" to specialize in clam and fish chowder and fish of all kinds. About two weeks later, a man named George Herman, identified as a Coney Island restaurant man, was arrested for the illegal sale of liquor, an action that would become common under Prohibition. Other small businesses were opening, especially at the south end. One place near the south end had been sold only five days after it opened because of the demand.

On December 9, the Sunshine Inn gave a banquet for 80 guests from the National Farms Estate (NFE) of Moore Haven, Florida, a group that controlled a large portion of land near Lake Okeechobee. The trip from Moore Haven to Miami Beach was part of a package for the group and, on Sunday, December 19, the NFE returned to the Sunshine Inn cafe for the fourth time that season.

A restaurant that opened near the end of 1920, on December 4, would be the only long-lasting survivor of restaurants, becoming an institution in Miami Beach. Until 1913, Joe Weiss had been a waiter and his wife, Jennie, had been a cook at small restaurants in New York. In 1913, Joe moved to the Miami area because of asthma and soon opened a lunch stand at Smith's Casino in Miami

Beach. In 1920, Joe Weiss had managed the Sunshine Inn, inside Smith's Casino, and had public mentions on at least two occasions. On July 22, the *Miami Metropolis* reported that, with G.A. Gloor as proprietor and Joe Weiss managing, the Sunshine Inn was the scene of "an excellent banquet which Joe Weiss, manager of the Sunshine Inn," had served to hungry mortals. The Miami Beach City Council minutes reported on September 15 that the city council had voted to pay a bill due to Joe Weiss for $9 for election dinners. On November 11, the *Metropolis* announced that the Sunshine Inn had been leased by Regello Duran, a Cuban restaurateur of long standing in Havana. The newspaper stated that Weiss would remain as chef "maintaining its high standards," but, only eight days later, a news item noted that Joe Weiss, formerly at the Sunshine Inn, would soon open a dining room at 213 Biscayne Avenue.

On December 4, 1920, after being a chef for seven years and after leaving the Sunshine Inn, apparently because of a change in management, Joe Weiss opened his own restaurant. The *Miami Metropolis* in "Decorates Lunchroom With a Hundred Flags" explained the reasons for starting Joe's:

> Joe Weiss has opened his own public dining room at 213 Biscayne avenue, one door from Collins avenue. One day Joe disappeared after having been chef at Sunshine inn for two [*sic*] years. Men who went there for fish dinners clamored for their favorite cook. They sought him out and induced Joe, who was taking a rest, to open a restaurant. The demands of Joe's friends have resulted in the latest eating place at the

The original Joe's Restaurant, with Joe and Jennie Weiss standing in front, remains an institution in Miami Beach as Joe's Stone Crab Restaurant.

Work on the Flamingo Hotel was a major news event in 1920. Carl Fisher was usually able to obtain concrete when many other developers were unable to get it because of shortages.

beach . . . Outside is a blazing sign, "Joe's," which tells the story to lots of men who have been sitting at Joe's tables for years. Fred Holliday will be head waiter.[3]

The *Miami Metropolis* in 1920 probably had no idea how important Joe's would become to Miami Beach, one of the few businesses to remain for decades until the present time, but the *Metropolis* went on to describe specific characteristics of the new restaurant. On December 16, another news item reported that G.J. McCann had completed changes at Joe's, adding a 9-foot by 24-foot porch dining room, enclosed in glass, a new kitchen, and other conveniences. Joe and Jennie Weiss lived in the back of the bungalow that housed the restaurant. Joe cooked and Jennie ran the dining room. Another significant event happened the same day that Joe's opened when Miami Beach's first post office opened on December 4, giving the city its first "Miami Beach" mailing address.

Another significant event would follow in just 27 days. The official opening date of the Flamingo Hotel, Miami Beach's first large luxury hotel, is generally considered to be January 1, 1921, but it actually opened to an invited group for its first social activity on December 31, 1920. The building of the Flamingo Hotel, with frequent progress reports, was a major news event in 1920. Carl Fisher was an extremely practical person and he certainly was aware of the desire of the newly wealthy industrial capitalists to be extravagant. In 1899, the sociologist Thorstein Veblen, in *The Theory of the Leisure Class*, had popularized the concepts of conspicuous leisure and conspicuous consumption, the notion that people did things to impress others. Fisher was an ardent reader and perhaps he had read Veblen, but, regardless, he certainly had a business understanding of the concept and how it could be used for his benefit in building his playground for the wealthy. The Flamingo Hotel would be a luxury hotel, although not as luxurious as some other hotels in resort areas throughout the United States. Fisher knew exactly what he wanted. Palm Beach was considered "stuffy," and Fisher was more interested in the "new money" of the northern and Great Lakes industrialists. The Flamingo Hotel would be luxurious enough to entice his customers to indulge in even more conspicuous consumption leisure activities, but also keep them in town long enough to interest them in buying property in Miami Beach.

On January 6, 1920, the *Miami Metropolis* reported that staking off the grounds for the foundation for the Flamingo Hotel had begun, and that construction was planned to begin in a few days. The scheduled completion date was the first of December. Plans called for a fireproof building, including a central tower 11 stories high, 200 rooms, each with bath, and 20 or more separate cottages. The main tower would include spacious public rooms for socializing and dining, several shops, a broker's office, a barbershop and manicure parlor, a modern laundry, and a refrigerating plant. Each of the rooms would face either the bay or the ocean.

Surrounded by attractive grounds and gardens, several tennis courts, and a golf putting course, the Flamingo Hotel was located on Biscayne Bay at the end of Fifteenth Street, in the "very heart" of the Alton Beach Development, close to golf courses, polo fields, bathing beaches, and casinos. One journalist wrote the following about the hotel:

> It was to have a wonderful view of the bay with Belle Isle and Star Island in the foreground. Extensive porches overlooking the bay will afford a fine opportunity to view yachts up and down the bay, a sight always interesting. A fine Pier will extend directly in front of the hotel where boats may anchor, and the Flamingo is sure to be a rendezvous for many yachting parties.[4]

On January 21, the city council gave Fisher's company permission to lay and maintain a 6-inch water main to the Flamingo's property line at the company's expense and agreed to purchase the line for the city within 10 years. By April 1920, Fisher had decided to build only six cottages, instead of the 20 or more originally planned. Cecil Fowler, vice president of the Flamingo Hotel, wanted wood cottages, but Fisher said that the area was very hard on paint and that it was better to use stucco than to have to repaint wood every season. On April 28, 1920, after 300 men had been making and raising forms for the Flamingo for three weeks, concrete was poured into the forms for the first floor. By May 1920, not less than 1,850 workers were on the payrolls of Carl Fisher and his associates, with about 1,650 of these actually working on the beach. The Flamingo Hotel was a major project but only part of Miami Beach's tremendous construction growth.

Several workers at the Flamingo Hotel narrowly escaped serious injury, if not death, on May 13, 1920 when the big derrick used for unloading barges suddenly toppled into the bay. A road roller had been tampered with a few days earlier and accusations were made that the tamperings might have happened because all the construction work was being done on the open-shop basis.

Construction in Miami Beach in 1920 was frequently delayed because building supplies, especially cement, were difficult to obtain and receive on time. By July, about half of the construction in Miami Beach and Miami had stopped or drastically slowed down because of the cement shortage, but the Flamingo Hotel construction was continuing because the builders had wisely contracted in advance for cement. The Miami Chamber of Commerce had requested, without success, that empty freight cars passing through on their way to Cuba be used to bring cement, but railroad owners had successfully objected because this would delay them getting to Cuba. There was a nationwide shortage of cars; in fact, over 2,500 United States cars were being used on Cuban railroads and could not be returned to relieve the shortage. Despite political turmoil over the presidential election, Havana was going through a building boom even greater than the Miami area.

Two-decade-old grapefruit, orange, and mandarin trees were planted in August. Potted plants and flowering shrubs that bloomed from November to March were also being planned. Foundations were down for the clay tennis courts, parkways were beginning to take shape, and two bungalows were being built to form part of the outdoor art by the eastern gardens. A system of exterior lights to outline the hotel at night was also installed, with the idea that the general illumination of the hotel would be a "splendid" advertisement.

On Saturday, September 11, 1920, after watching the unfurling of a 9-foot by 15-foot United States flag at the Flamingo, the *Miami Metropolis* gushed with praise for the great structure, gigantic in size and superb in architectural design. On October 9, the *Metropolis* had a "Flamingo Section," in which it described the hotel as the finest in Florida and a pleasant place to break the transcontinental trip to Cuba.

Charles S. Krom, the manager of the hotel, arrived in early November personally to see to the placing of the furnishings, carpets, and decorations. John Wanamaker, the prominent New York City specialist in interior furnishings, who had just finished furnishing and decorating the expanded Lincoln Hotel, was selected to fill the hotel's needs. David Mayer of Miami Beach, at his plant near the Purdy Boat Works, made 100 tables.

The shops and services available in the Flamingo Hotel were scheduled to be Black, Starr and Frostt, a leading Fifth Avenue jeweler; Bonwit Teller and Company, women's hats and gowns from Fifth Avenue, New York City; Don Ferris, men's haberdasher; Thomson and McKinnon, broker's office and member of New York and Chicago exchanges; Max Littwitz, laces and linens from New

Dancing in the Tea Garden,
Hotel Flamingo,
Miami, Fla.—24

The Flamingo Hotel's Tea Garden was a popular part of social life. The hotel's grand entrance was on the east side at the end of Fifteenth Street, but the Biscayne Bay (west) side was popular for social events.

York City; Isabel Spencer, hairdressing and manicuring; Jacob Opladen, barber shop and chiropody; Dr. O.F. Allen of Miami, house physician; Murphy Cycle Company, bicycles and wheel chairs; and a cigar and news stand with a full line of novelties and souvenirs.

On December 2, 1920, the Flamingo Hotel had electricity hooked up by the Miami Beach Electric Company, which Fisher had built because the Miami Electric Light and Power Company's electric current was inadequate and had arrived at Miami Beach (if it arrived) in fits and starts and at high prices. A few construction workers were doing odd jobs, but "the big job which tested the mettle of many men all through the long hot summer" was finished. The only big job remaining was unstacking and placing the furniture. The *Miami Metropolis* reported that dull blue or tan were the colors for carpets, beds, dressers, chairs, and dressing tables, with touches of details of mahogany on the beds and chairs, all harmonized with the old ivory walls. The great lounge was done in light yellow with the large square floor tiles being black and yellow. The sunroom was in reseda green with soft green draperies, plus furnishings done in flamingo pink and dull blue.

Awnings were also put up. Bamboo sprouts and tea bushes were planted about the Japanese teahouse. Main avenues, sidewalks, and tennis courts were being completed. The pavilion at the docks had been started and slips were deep enough and ready for yachts. A tennis shop had seemingly sprung up like a mushroom, the rock roads were oiled, and the oil-burning boilers had been given their first test.

In early December, Fisher was excited about the gondolas he was having built for the hotel. He wrote the following to John Oliver LaGorce:

> I had Purdy come down on a rush order and we are going to build six of them in twenty days. I have some of the most wonderful Bahama negroes you ever saw to push these gondolas around. They are all going to be stripped to the waist and wear big brass ear rings. And possibly necklaces of live crabs on crawfish. Too bad you can't say anything about this in the front pages of the *Saturday Evening Post*, but I really believe it will be alright.[5]

Fisher was probably referring to Edward D. Purdy, father of several children and president of Purdy Boat Company, which was located on Biscayne Bay near Eighteenth Street in Miami Beach. Purdy was a native of Canada who had come to the United States in 1885 and lived in Trenton, Michigan when the 1920 census was taken. He described himself as a builder of pleasure boats. Also working at Purdy Boat Company was Robert C. Purdy, a boat builder, and George W. Purdy, a carpenter.

As the opening date neared, frequent progress reports were published. A children's playground was being constructed. A large yellow fence was erected

Blacks, mostly from the southern United States or the Bahamas, were a major force in the building of the Flamingo Hotel in 1920.

Shown here are the famous Bahamians who pushed the gondolas in Biscayne Bay, with the Flamingo Hotel in the background.

across the front of the entrance drive, shutting out visitors from the grounds. The hotel was attracting much attention and hundreds of cars had been driven to the entrance out of curiosity.

On December 19, 1920, the Flamingo Hotel announced in the *Miami Herald* that it would open on January 1, 1921 with the opening dinner held that evening. However, because of the demand for the New Year's dinner, there would be an "invitation only" formal dinner and reception on New Year's Eve. The Flamingo Hotel opening was expected to mark a new era in the history of Miami Beach and Miami, adding incalculably to the prestige of Miami Beach and Miami's social life. Including afternoon tea and garden dances, the Flamingo Hotel was predicted to be Miami Beach's center of social life. The hotel was already booked for January and February.

On December 26, 1920, the Sunday before the opening, tourists and travelers clamored all day for permission to take a look at the hotel, but neither coaxing or attempted bribes could get people admitted. A few finishing touches were being completed. Sixteen men were connecting telephones and setting up the switchboard. Louis Agassiz Fuertes was on his way from Ithaca, New York with mural paintings for the lounge. A local news piece reported that the flamingos, the beautiful seabirds from which Fisher had chosen the name for his hotel, would be used in the mural decorations for the lounge. Fuertes had gone to the Andros Islands in the Bahamas, about 135 miles southeast of Miami Beach, in the spring to make studies of the live flamingos in color and had reproduced a frieze to be placed over the great fireplace in the lounge.

This view shows Belle Isle after the last link connecting it to Miami Beach was completed. Note the Flamingo Hotel in the background to the south.

Fisher had received strong opposition against the murals from both his manager and Cecil Fowler. Fowler had written to Fisher, saying that he had talked to prominent Chicago architects, artists, and mural decorators, and that they all thought the flamingos should be paintings hung on walls rather than wall murals. Fisher responded to Fowler that LaGorce of *National Geographic* and Fuertes agreed with having the murals. The spat continued. Fowler wrote back to Fisher that LaGorce and Fuertes were artists, but not architects, and that the Wanamaker decorating department also thought that murals were not appropriate for the Flamingo Hotel. Fisher then ended the debate by writing Fowler that LaGorce and Fuertes were artistic people who knew about such things. Fisher got his way on most things—this instance was no exception. He listened to other opinions, but, after all, he was the boss. Fisher also criticized the prominent Chicago architect whom Fowler had referenced, saying that this architect had designed the "damndest" stairway entrance for the Flamingo, an entrance that looked like the back stairs to a rat's cellar. Fisher noted that he had another stairway designed that was 40 or 50 feet wide and looked like a place to enter.

Work continued on the finishing touches for the opening of the hotel. "Burly men with bulging muscles" rolled pianos into the Flamingo Hotel. Mail was already coming for prospective guests. Gallons of rich Guernsey milk and bottles of cream had been received from Broad Ripple Farm, the Fisher-owned farm in Miami Beach on the north side of today's Forty-first Street near Prairie Avenue. The first names on the Flamingo's register were those of a prestigious party from

Washington, New York, and Philadelphia, including Reinald Werrenrath, the celebrated baritone of the Metropolitan Opera; Fuertes, the famous painter of wildlife who had done the murals; and LaGorce from Washington, D.C., managing editor of *National Geographic Magazine*.

So, not only did Carl Fisher's drive get the hotel ready for its January 1 goal, but it actually held its first public event on the last day of 1920. While the January 1 dinner and reception was referred to as the formal opening, the December 31 dinner and reception was referred to as a "Housewarming." Mr. and Mrs. Fisher had 25 people at their table and about 200 total attendees. About 180 people were listed by name in the *Miami Herald*.

In October, one of Carl Fisher's managers, F.R. Humpage, reported to Fisher that the people in Miami were making favorable comments about the Flamingo's completion, saying that Fisher had a reputation for finishing what he started. Indeed, to build such a hotel in such a short period of time was a tremendous feat. Fisher's original partner, James A. Allison, had dropped out when the price went higher than expected. There was a national post-war construction boom, which was leading to higher prices for labor and supplies and Fisher had argued with, and replaced, his original designer of the hotel. Fisher acknowledged to the designer that the hotel was not going to be as fancy or expensive as the designer planned, but that it was going to be what Fisher had tried to say he wanted. The final cost Fisher publicized was $1.25 million without the grounds and he estimated earnings of $125,000 to $150,000 per season.

Decades later, Ann Armbruster wrote that, from a modern perspective, the Flamingo Hotel was an austere and hulking building, but that its lack of architectural distinction was made up for by its variety. Indeed, Fisher was a

This souvenir postcard shows the controversial mural in the Flamingo Hotel lounge. Fisher named the hotel after the pink flamingos that he had brought from the Bahamas.

consummate business and financial planner, and he had the right mixture of cost and design for Miami Beach in 1920. There were grander hotels elsewhere, but, as noted, Fisher's major goal was not to attract tourists but to attract and impress potential buyers for future home sites. Pushing to get the hotel opened during the height of the winter season helped the hotel to become an instant success. As Howard Kleinberg showed in his excellent book, Fisher also was a master at good publicity.

In July 1920, Charles Krom had written to Fisher, saying that he agreed that the Flamingo should get high rates, but that they had to be careful not to charge too much in the first year since people did not know the hotel. Krom had looked at prices at other hotels and suggested a minimum rate of $15 per day even for the tenth-floor rooms without baths, $16 to $22 per day for a single room and bath for two persons, and $30 to $40 per day for a double room and bath for two persons.

Fisher wrote on May 6, 1921 that the hotel and the cottages had been very successful. The hotel was already 85-percent booked for the coming season and over 2,200 people had already been turned away by February. Carl Fisher had his suite and offices on the eighth floor. The Flamingo Hotel and all its surroundings were a central part of Fisher's dreams of a luxurious winter resort. As 1920 ended and 1921 began, Miami Beach had entered a new era in hotels and other tourist attractions. Things would never be the same again. Miami Beach was beginning to bloom!

This postcard view, looking east from Biscayne Bay toward the Atlantic Ocean, is entitled "Beautiful Flamingo Hotel and Surroundings, Miami, Fla." Then, as now, Miami sometimes was mistakenly given credit for Miami Beach accomplishments.

6. Casinos and Baths

Because of their location on the ocean and their attraction to Miami mainland residents, casinos and bathhouses got an early start on the peninsula that later became Miami Beach. A one-room shack had been built on the Lum property in 1901 and was occasionally rented to Miamians for a week or so, but the first real casino was built in 1904 by Richard S. Smith of Hartford, Connecticut.

Avery C. Smith (no relation to Richard) came to the Miami area from Connecticut in 1908, went back to Connecticut, returned to Miami and Miami Beach with a partner, and had started building boats and wharves at Miami and the beach by 1909, as well as bathhouses and boardwalks. Avery Smith bought the abandoned Richard S. Smith building, a two-story pavilion located on the south side of Biscayne Avenue (South Pointe Drive) at the end of Ocean Drive. First known as Fairy-Land, it became well known as Smith's Casino. As Biscayne Navigation Company, Smith operated boats (including the *Lady Lou*, *Sallie*, *Mauretania*, and *Lusitania*), ferrying passengers from Miami to Miami Beach, and interrelated his two businesses to make Smith's Casino a popular destination. Passengers landed on the Biscayne Bay (west) side of the peninsula, and walked across a 6-foot-wide, 550-foot-long wooden boardwalk to Smith's Casino on the Atlantic Ocean (east) side of the peninsula.

In about 1913, the Collins Pavilion, later known as the Miami Beach Casino, was built of driftwood by the Pancoasts on the ocean at Twenty-third Street. They added a swimming pool in 1914 and, in 1916, sold it to Fisher, who then improved it. Dan Hardie, the sheriff of Dade County from 1909 to 1917, built a more pretentious bathhouse than Smith's, known as Hardie's Casino, in 1914. It was located on the east side of Ocean Drive, a little north of Biscayne Avenue and in front of today's Penrod's. It was also known as the Ocean Beach Amusement Company.

Not only did the casinos and bathhouses precede the city and other social activities, but they remained popular, especially with local residents and local county visitors, despite all the glitter that developed in the city. In 1920, the Miami Beach Casino, Miami Beach Baths, Hardie's Casino, and Smith's Casino were major centers of social life in the little city. The three casinos also advertised in the city directory as baths.

All of these establishments were mentioned frequently in local newspaper articles throughout the year and through these, we can get a good overview of the city's social life in these establishments. These were not gambling casinos, but were for social purposes, such as dancing, swimming, and eating.

On New Year's Day 1920, the New Year's Eve dinner dance at the Miami Beach Casino was considered the most successful event of its kind ever given in Miami Beach. The combination of the Ray Manderson Orchestra, decorations, Greta Hardough's dining, and a luxurious ballroom, one of the largest in the South, produced a brilliant evening. Christmas and New Year's regalia were left up through Saturday night's dance on January 3, 1920, so that those who missed the decorations could still view them. After the holidays were over, dancing was scheduled for Tuesday, Thursday, and Saturday nights, with music and dancing every day during the hours that luncheon was served. At the first Tuesday night dance, many young people participated and were complimented on how much they had learned at Kathryn Stafford's dancing studio at the casino. It was felt that even if the casino was open every night for dancing, as planned, it would be busy. There were many visitors from Miami.

There was a cold snap for several days in early January, but at the first signs of warm sunshine on January 7, people flocked to Miami Beach, with many swimmers and bathers at the casinos. Meanwhile, the dances at the Miami Beach Casino were growing more popular with people who came "from the frozen north." The casino gained the reputation of meeting the demands of the most fastidious winter tourists. A Sunday afternoon concert was introduced. A special à la carte dinner was begun at 6:30, before dancing at 8 p.m., and soon Saturday nights became known as "chicken and waffle dinner" night. Monday nights were reserved for the weekly dance of the Monday Dancing Club, an exclusive club with over 100 members. A Sunday afternoon tea was also very popular.

Fashion was important and newspapers made frequent comments about many women in stunning costumes, with detailed discussions of designs and colors. Women's bathing suits were important, although sometimes controversial. The long-sleeved and high-necked bathing suits popular at Palm Beach were being introduced in Miami Beach, and were praised for protecting shoulders and arms from sunburn while not hindering swimming. The suits were popular in Palm Beach by those who wanted to preserve white arms and shoulders for decolleté occasions (where women wore low-necked gowns). In February, the Miami Beach Casino had three special events: a moon dance for Valentine's Day, a Washington's Birthday celebration on February 22, and an original dance from the Arabian Nights' Entertainment on February 28.

At the St. Valentine's dance, over 250 people made reservations for dinner and over 150 were turned down. The *Miami Metropolis* wrote that a large moon shone down on the dancers during the waltzing and lights were dimmed for some of the dances so that "only the romantic old moon" radiated over the crowd. For Washington's Birthday, a large and brilliant ball was held the night of February 21.

Excursion Boats, Miami. Fla.

This postcard shows the Mauretania *and the* Lusitania, *two of Avery Smith's excursion boats that brought people to Smith's Casino. Smith's boating business was known as the Biscayne Navigation Company.*

The ballroom was decorated in red, white, and blue, with Old Glory and stars and stripes everywhere.

At the Arabian Nights ball, a few people wore Oriental costumes, and music and decorations followed the same theme. Costumes were encouraged, but most society members "lazily" decided to wear evening dresses, though some compromised by wearing Oriental headdress. Kathryn and Irene Stafford, hostesses at the casino, wore Egyptian dancing costumes, and Mary Lang was dressed as a Geisha girl, keeping the guests supplied with cigarettes from her tray. With the usual glowing comments, the *Miami Herald* called the ball the most magnificent affair ever held at the beach. Miami Beach received very good publicity, partly because it really did have outstanding activities and partly because of Carl Fisher's skills.

Meanwhile, the Miami Beach Baths, next door to the Miami Beach Casino, was having its own special events. On Washington's Birthday, a record crowd attended a water carnival, including a 100-yard dash and a one-half-mile race (18 lengths of the pool). Miami Beach resident J. Newton Lummus Jr., son of Miami Beach's first mayor and a future mayor himself (December 1926 to December 1928), came in second. Frances Bilsbarrow and Blanch Everley, the first and third place winners in the New Year's cross-bay swim, also gave an exhibition.

While most attention was given to the Miami Beach Casino, both Hardie's Casino and Smith's Casino also were busy. A trapshooting, the second of the

This bird's-eye view of the Miami Beach Casino, frequently referred to as Fisher's Casino, shows the casino from the air above the ocean.

season, was held on January 14 at the Miami Gun Club's traps on the oceanfront, a short distance north of Hardie's Casino. Shoots were planned for each week during the winter. A week later, it was reported that there had been an enthusiastic gathering at another trapshooting. In December 1920, Ellis G. King, manager of Miami Beach's new trolley system, and Captain Frank H. Henning, a new city councilman, were reported as doing some of the best rifle shooting at the American rifle range on Ocean Drive.

Many activities also continued at Hardie's and Smith's. On January 25, 1920, about 30 Boy Scouts from Miami's Troop Number 8 hiked over to Miami Beach early in the morning and spent the day at Smith's Casino enjoying "all the pleasures that a bunch of youngsters at the seashore could enjoy." A big truck returned them home in the late afternoon. Many Kansas tourists, as well as former Kansas residents living in Dade and Broward Counties, attended a Kansas Day picnic at Smith's Casino at the end of January.

In February 1920, Hardie's Casino had been almost entirely remodeled. A tiled passageway led through the casino to an arcade on the ocean side where offices were located and where there was access to the bathhouses, including an additional 200. There were shops on both the ocean side and the Ocean Drive side. A recently enlarged ballroom was on the second floor, and the old restaurant had been torn away and replaced by a restaurant on the west side of the second floor. Dan Hardie also announced plans to build an amusement park covering 14 city lots, between Atlantic Boulevard (Collins Avenue) and Ocean Drive, and the newspapers noted that rollercoasters and other fun-making novelties were about the only things needed to have a complete resort.

Hardie's held Tuesday night affairs and Thursday night dances with a "smoothness of floor and sweep of breeze" in its magnificent ballroom with excellent jazz music. Thursday afternoons saw the growing popularity of its dance classes. Canoes and surf coasters had become very popular and the restaurant, under the management of Leon DeLeon, provided excellent refreshments. Visitors could have a complete day at Hardie's.

On Saturday, February 21, Hardie's Casino was the site of a Blue and Grey picnic for veterans of both sides of the Civil War. Over 500 veterans and guests attended. The occasion was such a success that it was decided to form a permanent organization and a ladies' auxiliary, and make the picnic an annual affair. Over 100 automobiles, which had been solicited in the newspaper, conveyed the veterans and their families to the beach after a send-off from the front of the Royal Palm Hotel in downtown Miami. Over 1,000 people were seated and others stood in Hardie's ballroom for a program.

February had been a very good month for the casinos and baths. A period of rainy weather in the middle of the month had mixed effects, but the newspaper noted that there were many bathers, mostly ladies, despite the rain. At the end of the month, it was noted that the weather had been ideal for bathers for the last few days, and that the Miami Beach Casino, Hardie's Casino, and Smith's Casino had enjoyed record crowds. The opening of the County Causeway on February 17, 1920 had made Hardie's Casino and Smith's Casino very convenient for people from Miami and the mainland. Larger crowds than ever were visiting the south end of the city. Meanwhile, the Miami Beach Social Club continued to take over the Miami Beach Casino on Monday nights for dances.

The year 1920 was a leap year and a Sunday morning parade on February 29 brought the busy month to a successful close. The *Miami Herald* described the day as life at its gayest at Miami Beach. An article entitled "Sunday Morning Parade Brought Brilliant Assemblage to Casinos at Miami Beach" gave an accurate view of leisure and fashion in Miami Beach, and mentioned many people involved in the city's society life.

The exciting and hectic pace continued in March. In the early part of the month, a policeman in Miami noticed two men driving a car that had been stolen in Jacksonville, Florida and tailed it to Smith's Casino. The men parked the car at the casino and went into a tent to the south of the building. A search for the men soon led to a chase, with Chief Brogdon of Miami Beach chasing one of the men into former Sheriff Dan Hardie's backyard where the car thief ran into Hardie's arms just as Brogdon was about to grab him. The other car thief got to the dock, seized a rowboat, and went into the bay. Brogdon did not have a weapon, so he rushed into the office of the Gulf Refining Company to get a pistol, got a ride from a friendly tugboat captain whose boat was at the dock, and gave chase. The tugboat rapidly outran the thief's rowboat and the thief was captured.

Hardie's Casino started vaudeville sketches on Thursday nights with the Rickerts, a group well known in Miami, playing four vaudeville acts during each dance evening. Hardie's was the scene of another large picnic when several hundred Ohio folk brought bountiful baskets and reveled in memories of their home state.

The Miami Beach Casino hosted the winners of the Mid-winter Regatta and the members of the Cuban polo teams during March. The *Miami Metropolis* noted that the major feature at the beach was the Cuban army officers, who had recently finished the polo match. The dance for the Cuban visitors vied with the St. Patrick's Day Dance for the chief event in Miami Beach in mid-March. The Miami Beach Casino pools periodically had swimming races and exhibitions. The pools at the casinos continued to be popular even on March days, despite the wind blowing at the "proverbial forty knots an hour."

Despite his many enterprises, Fisher continued his concern with small details by writing J. Arthur Pancoast, manager of the Miami Beach Baths, that something had to be done immediately at the beach to protect the chairs that that were being used in the afternoons by loafers who were not paying. Fisher complained that the loafers did more damage to the chairs than the people that paid during the noon hour.

By March 22, 1920, the *Miami Metropolis* noted that the season was well advanced, but that the Miami Beach Casino dance was still so popular that it reminded one of the mid-season affairs. It was evident that the winter season was getting longer and that the Miami Beach Casino would have regular dances until about April 15. Visitors and Miamians were fairly haunting the beach, trying to get more fun in before April 15. Hardie's and Smith's, of course, would continue to boom all summer.

Hardie's continued to advertise its Thursday night dances at $1.10 per couple. Crowds kept getting larger at the Thursday night dances, and Hardie's Sunday afternoon concerts were very popular because the casino was a convenient Sunday afternoon drive. Swimming at night also remained a popular summer diversion.

At the end of March, the last major tourist event of the season at the Miami Beach Casino was a luncheon for the Florida State Hotel Association Convention. Over 200 New England delegates and many others attended the event hosted by Carl Fisher. The president of the association assured Miami Beach that the members would be great advertisers for Miami Beach, and that "all would return full of praise of this wonder spot of the south." Carl Fisher had chalked up yet another publicity success.

By the first of April, newspaper attention given to the social activities of tourists abruptly decreased to almost none. Tourists had remained longer than usual, hundreds of them now were leaving by cars, and most of the notices were listings of winter residents who were going back north. On Saturday night, April 3, the Miami Beach Casino's dance was a huge success, with many prominent visitors hosting large going away parties for friends. There also were local special parties, exemplified by the senior class from Miami High School, which played and roasted wieners on the beach and later danced at the Miami Beach Casino.

Hardie's Casino continued to host the L.P. Club, a social group of 40 young men, on Sunday afternoons. No one knew what the letters stood for, so the bathing public at Hardie's dubbed them a "lotta prunes." The club's initiation for new members was a very active and rambunctious affair in the surf in front of Hardie's Casino. The club's goal was to promote good fellowship, develop innocent sports, and "indulge social features." The largest attendance ever recorded at Hardie's Casino took place on April 4, 1920 with the L.P. Club and their guests having strenuous games of basketball, horse fights, volleyball, merry-go-round, passing the medicine ball, pyramid building, trapeze and slack-wire work, and fancy diving and other water sports in the pool. The men announced that they would not be at Hardie's the following Sunday because they were taking their girlfriends on a "straw-ride" to Fort Lauderdale and its beach.

Finally, with mixed feelings about the ending of the season, the Miami Beach Casino had its farewell ball on Saturday night, April 10, and a season of "unprecedented gaiety and brilliance" was brought to a successful close. Farewells were said to the highly acclaimed Ray Manderson Orchestra and to numerous workers at the casino. The season finally had officially ended.

By April 16, the *Miami Herald*, noting that the tourists were all gone or going, would write "Miami Settling Down to Enjoy Summer Days." The popular Thursday half-holiday, whereby many stores closed at noon on Thursdays, had begun for grocery stores and meat markets. Clerks and storekeepers flocked to the beaches and Tamiami Trail to watch the dredging for the road, as well as taking airplane rides and automobile rides into the surrounding countryside. However,

This photo shows the front (west) side of Hardie's Casino on Ocean Drive. The casino, located in front of today's famous Penrod's, was a major attraction on South Beach.

so many people still went to the beaches that the causeway was lined with automobiles for a long time. By early May, the half-holiday was extended to almost all retail stores, and garages and auto accessory places would close at 1 p.m. Half-holidays would last until early September.

Fisher considered selling his casino, decided against it, and announced that it would be completely remodeled over the summer and operated as a private club in the next season. The opening of the Flamingo Hotel would replace much of the social life that had taken place at the casino, but to turn it into a private club, plans were made for an addition of large entrance stairways, a lounging place for men, additional facilities for women, a smoking room, and two more shops. The papers reported that the Ray Manderson Orchestra would return for the next season. Manderson had just returned from Cuba where he had been sent by Fisher to look for a Cuban orchestra to bring to Miami Beach for the next season and to add to the music. Apparently, Manderson was not successful.

Fisher also considered selling some land north of James Snowden's property at Forty-fourth Street on Collins Avenue for a small club, but was concerned that the club might be interested in gambling. Fisher had a strong opposition to gambling. His wife, Jane, wrote much later that although he patronized the local bootleggers, he feared and hated the professional gamblers because of what they might do to his dream city.

Avery C. Smith had given a contract to enlarge his casino by late April, but also announced that the casino would stay open until 10:30 every night except

Hardie's Casino, with a front on Ocean Drive, had a swimming pool on the north side of the casino, with the east end of the pool facing the Atlantic Ocean. Hardie's was also known as the Ocean Beach Amusement Company.

Saturday and Sunday, while the bathhouses would close at 6 p.m. Smith's addition was to be to the east front of his bathhouse, and the addition would contain about 200 rooms, bringing Smith's total number to 700. Because the addition would extend to within 10 feet of the high watermark and because of heavy winds at times, Smith planned to construct a piling foundation. The addition would give Smith a lengthy total of 324 feet of building frontage on Biscayne Avenue.

The summer was enjoyed at the casinos with a few major events and many small events. For example, the Trinity Episcopal Church Sunday School held its annual picnic at Smith's Casino in May. Hardie's had a small fire in its east balcony in late May. Luckily, a night police officer detected smoke pouring from the entrance to Hardie's Casino and extinguished the fire with pails of water. It was thought that the fire began with a cigar dropped in a cushioned chair and thanks were given that there had not been a strong northern wind that night.

About 200 young people from Miami, Coconut Grove, Lemon City, and Fort Lauderdale enjoyed a lively June dance at Hardie's and, on June 7, 1920, a number of young people from Miami rode over to Smith's Casino for an evening of fun. Hardie's Casino hosted one of the largest dances of the season on June 11 with a cool breeze that sprang up during the afternoon, giving the right temperature for the devotees of the jazz.

On Tuesday, June 15, the *Miami Metropolis* reported a "a day at the beach" in detail and, taking sides against the movement to maintain very conservative women's bathing suits, stated the following about the previous Sunday:

> Fantastic bathing suits appeared in numbers. Every color and combination imaginable walked the beach. The day of the satin bathing suit seems past. Ninety-nine percent of the women wore the Annette Kellerman suits and looked unconscious of the snugness of their fit . . . An early feature of the day was a sunrise breakfast which was served at the gun club where 10 Miamians partook of broiled bacon, toast and coffee prepared over a fire by a colored cook while the members of the party were in the sea.[1]

A large crowd watched a diving and swimming exhibition at Smith's by Joseph Hovelsrud, who taught swimming in Havana during the winter, and William J. Brown Jr., son of the Brown's Hotel owners. Also in mid-June, several local church groups had picnics at different casinos on the beach.

According to the *Miami Herald*, everyone went to Hardie's on Thursday half-holidays, where the bathing beach was unsurpassed in the country. Over 400 bathhouses "of the best" were provided, but they were not enough for Thursdays and Sundays. Hardie's had a "veritable children's delight" with a wonderful beach, seesaws, swings, and merry-go-rounds. Both Hardie's Casino and Smith's Casino were reported as doing a roaring trade on half-Thursdays.

In the last weeks of June, the Miami Beach Baths started opening every evening except Sunday because of demand. However, a week later, it was announced that the baths would be closing for the rest of the summer so the facilities could be remodeled and enlarged for the much-talked-about conversion to a private club for November's scheduled opening. New showers and other improvements were planned.

The baths could survive during the summer only by reducing prices to get volume business. Hardie's charged 25¢ to 35¢ to parties owning their bathing suits, and 50¢ to 60¢ when suits were furnished. Smith's charged 15¢ for a room, and 25¢ for a room and a suit. Also, J. Arthur Pancoast, the manager, was in poor health, so Fisher decided not to compete with Hardie's and Smith's lower rates.

Independence Day was celebrated at Hardie's with much patriotic decorating on Monday, July 5, because July 4 was a Sunday. In general, Miami and Miami Beach's celebrations were "safe and sane" with no parades, oratory, or fireworks. A baseball game in Miami, a boxing match at Elser Pier in Miami, and picnics at Miami Beach were the main happenings. The *Miami Daily Metropolis* noted that the beach seemed to be the mecca for most, that the record of automobiles crossing the causeway probably would be broken, and that police would be enforcing speed limits.

With a half-holiday and "the delightful facilities for pleasure" that Hardie's and Smith's provided, it was another big day at Miami Beach. Pontoons had become popular among Hardie's bathers. One visitor was struck by a hydroairplane pontoon being used by a bather, but he "pluckily made light" of the accident. Nevertheless, lifeguards prohibited further use of pontoons because of the large number of bathers.

Despite all the pleasurable attributes of the casinos, there were also negatives. About ten people—shopkeepers, restaurateurs, and men-about-town—lost money in May to a glib-talking swindler. Dressed in fashionable clothes, staying at the Olive Apartments, and claiming to be the son of a rich New York man who was sending him money, the bunco game player disappeared after running up charges and bouncing checks in the south end. Police officers were called to Smith's Casino on June 11 to help trace some missing bathing suits, which were believed to have been taken to Miami by patrons, but it was noted that filching of bathing suits was decreasing. However, a watch and $8 were reported stolen in mid-July.

The casinos and other businesses in the south end were not the only targets for stealing. Early in the summer, there was an epidemic of theft on the beach, and houses in the north end of the city were broken into. In late November, Anne McSweeny, owner of a handsome house on Ocean Drive near Eleventh Street, returned for the winter and discovered that her home had been broken into sometime during the months she had been away at her residence in Pennsylvania. A $2,000 Dodge touring car had been stolen from her garage. About a week later, a man took a taxi to Miami Beach from Miami where he "had been celebrating the arrival of Christopher Columbus." After waiting for two hours for his passenger to return, the taxi driver notified the police and the man was found. The lost man claimed that he had fallen asleep on the sand and that his purse

This photo of the Allies Ball, held about 1920, shows the flag-decorated interior of the Miami Beach Casino.

containing $1,000 was missing. He offered the police a liberal reward and went back to Miami without his money, sadder but wiser, hopefully.

Other unwanted characters, referred to as human-biting mosquitoes, also continued to take away from the pleasures. Two schoolteachers, Marion and Mabel West of Washington, D.C., had hitchhiked south during the summer and were staying in their "dog" tent on the beach. They were writing a story of their tramp trip south to Miami Beach. Driven from their tent by the mosquitoes, they found refuge in the screened porch in I.M. Martin's bungalow on Ocean Drive.

Despite the problems, however, the good far outweighed the bad. On Sunday, July 25, for example, a typical Sunday at the beach in the casino area included a pilot with a hydroairplane, who charged passengers $10 for a flight over the ocean and the bay; an impromptu baseball team, which played with a cork ball; girls in brilliant bathing suits, who leapfrogged before a large male gallery; and camera fiends, who photographed just about everybody.

In early July, a controversial issue again got attention at Miami Beach. The *Miami Metropolis* reported the following:

> One-piece tights for bathing suits have made their appearance on the South Beach at bathing hours this week. The tights are without the skirts which are commonly known as the California style bathing suits. Both are single bathing garments, the later a combination of skirt and

The back (east) side of Hardie's Casino faced the Atlantic Ocean and was the site of much sun and fun.

tights. Bathing tights are prohibited at Long Beach, Atlantic City and other resorts.[2]

Some women bathers at the baths, casinos, and beaches felt excitement and apprehension during July when women's organizations in Miami "agitated" for more modest dress at the beach. The *Miami Metropolis* summarized the two positions, saying that no limit had been placed on the length of the single-piece bathing dresses worn by women and they were abbreviated to extremes. Some young women started wearing men's bathing suits, as snug as possible. The author wrote that sometimes the bathing apparel was very risky. Whether the writer meant risky or risque, or both, will probably never be known. After criticism, there was a notable change among the worst offenders, with some women going back to one-piece women's suits and some even wearing an overdress over swimming trunks.

A short time later, Mrs. Lura (Herman) Scheibli of 608 Collins Avenue, in a letter to the editor of the *Miami Metropolis*, chided those moralists who were upset at the human body, but also chided bathers who wore bathing suits to stores. She wrote that bathers had shocked neighborhoods with their merry laughter on Sabbath mornings and other days, and had been accused of dressing in immoral and improper attire, but that they were guilty only of bad judgment for having been seen in stores in town in bathing suits.

Helona Remington, in an article written exclusively for the *Miami Herald*, noted that, on August 15, the youth and middle-aged of Miami and its suburbs went to the beach in force in one-piece bathing suits. She wrote that the bathers did not care for the "outworn edicts of 19th century convention" and that fewer of the baggy, two-piece, old plough-horse women's models were seen. As for the male bathers, she wrote the following:

> The ladies may come, and the ladies may go, but the men, God bless 'em, they never change. No pink for them, no stockings, no fads that change with every ocean breeze . . . Some of them have their own suits which they keep at the beach for use when they can get across for a plunge now and then, but the majority use the same old rented ones that we have known for years, with the "H-A-R-D-I-E" or "S-M-I-T-H" stenciled in stiff whitewash across the front, or maybe across the back, because they often put 'em on wrong. No woman would do that, you bet![3]

Hardie's hosted a dance for the officers of the U.S.S. *Saterleg* on August 10 and, two days later, South Beach had what was described as its biggest Thursday afternoon of the summer with "more bathers, more boys, and more babies" than before. The boys were mostly Boy Scouts from Miami and Key West. Five black nurses formed a group at one beach with numerous babies in arms. The half-holiday ended with the usual Thursday evening dance at Hardie's with many young people from Miami.

The baths and casinos faced a potentially costly problem when, in mid-August, the city council took an interest in seeing that all bathing suits, towels, and other equipment used in baths and pools were sterilized and that the water in the swimming pools was changed at more frequent intervals. Avery C. Smith argued against the measure and the ordinance was delayed out of courtesy to Dan Hardie, who was traveling in Colorado. In August, the city council asked Avery Smith to allow the city fire engine to tap water out of his pool in case of an emergency, but the discussions got bogged down.

At about the same time that legal problems started for the baths and casinos, there were other concerns. In the early morning of Tuesday, August 4, a motorload of rowdies from Miami, drunk and disorderly, caused a crawl in the vicinity of the casinos. With cutouts open in their cars, they drove around and around in the area, keeping people away with boisterous behavior, and then climbed on the porch of the Lummus building and insulted guests at the Beach Inn. The disturbance continued for over two hours. On September 1, City Councilman Charles Meloy, who lived in the area near today's Rebecca Towers, suggested that places of business, such as restaurants, refreshment stands, and the like, where night joy-riders hung out, should be forced to close at midnight or at some set hour in order to help police maintain order.

Fisher also complained in a letter to Mayor Pancoast about problems at the Miami Beach Casino. Fisher had left his pier open to the public, but drunks were doing such things as tossing whiskey bottles all over the place and throwing dead fish on the settees. Fisher suggested to the mayor that the city should build a street down through the city park and erect a pier there. On September 1, the city council also heard complaints about garbage washing up on the beach at the south end and appointed a councilman to "see that garbage is dumped at sea, during the proper tide, in the future."

As August ended, local groups continued to celebrate activities in Miami Beach. A special visitor to the casinos on the half-holiday of Thursday, September 2 was Willie Willie of the Seminole tribe of Native Americans. The *Miami Metropolis* noted that he was wearing his customary flaming neckwear and high class haberdashery and that it had been "several moons" since the Seminole paid a visit to the casinos. Willie Willie had a village on the site of present-day Hialeah, about 9 miles from Miami Beach, until about 1929.

Smith's Casino was the central place of interest on Labor Day, with athletic stunts, a series of boxing matches, swimming, racing, and other sporting events for all ages and all physical conditions. Dancing, swings, slides, and the pool also provided fun. The plan was to make Smith's Casino the center of recreation for laboring people. No formal planning took place except for a barbecue, which the casino was to furnish in the afternoon. The planned barbecue at Smith's fell through, so people had to bring their own bulging baskets and bulky boxes.

The popularity of South Beach continued with the announcement in early September of plans to build a big dancing pavilion and tearoom on the ocean side of Ocean Drive between Second and Third Streets. Planned by Earl Brunswick of New York, the pavilion and tearoom was to give the effect of a log cabin, with part for people using the beach entrance and another part for people entering from Ocean Drive. Bathers would not be allowed to meet patrons entering in street dress. Japanese waiters dressed in costume to serve tea.

Joseph Fralinger of Pennsylvania wrote a letter that was read to the South End Club on September 27 in which he said that he and his wife controlled more (nine) lots on Ocean Drive than anybody else. The Fralingers strongly supported the idea of building a 24- to 30-foot-wide elevated boardwalk along the beach from First Street to Sixth Street, and they volunteered to donate 5 feet to widen Ocean Drive.

A special event was held at Hardie's in mid-September when two French artists, Professor and Madame Neckerson, gave a music and magic performance. Madame Neckerson sang, with accompaniment by Iva Sproule-Baker, a permanent Miami Beach resident. Professor Neckerson contributed legerdemain tricks and a variety of works of magic. The Neckersons, who had performed all over the world, were on their way to Panama. Andre de Monceaux, a native of France and a Miami Beach resident and policeman, managed the Neckersons' performance.

As Miami Beach began to think about its forthcoming city election in October, Smith's Casino was the site of important meetings of the South End Club, which was interested in the qualifications of candidates. By this time, Avery C. Smith had completed a new addition of 200 bathing rooms, bringing his total number of bathing rooms to about 700 and leading to the claim that Smith's Casino was the biggest bathhouse on the south Atlantic coast. The rooms, however, were small, basically for only changing clothes.

Despite all the activities, the *Miami Metropolis* claimed that there was even more late-night life in cafes and restaurants than was realized. With an article entitled "South Beach Night Life is Gay and Interesting: Moonlight Bathing Has Strong Attractions for Many," the *Miami Metropolis* wrote not only that restaurants were full, but also reported the following:

> There is a fascinating side to life at South Beach that many patrons never see. It is the night life in the cafes and restaurants. Then restaurants thrive and lights burn late and there is merriment and song and laughter. There is a fascination about night bathing and it has its regular followers: scantily clad figures race up and down the shore . . . As night lengthens, the life becomes more suggestive and mysterious. Big sedans pull up before a restaurant and women hurry within closely veiled; chauffeurs fall asleep in waiting machines; a dog barks loudly at some night walker; there is the machine-gun snapping of the police motorcycle, the distant crowing of chanticleer, and subdued mirth and shrill women's voices. Shortly, the last of the motor cars roll away. It is 2:30 a.m.[4]

The controversy over bathing suits continued with a different twist. Some people were changing their bathing suits in their cars because they could not, or would not, pay the price of a changing room for a family, and the city marshal was trying to change the practice. The *Miami Metropolis*, in a strong editorial entitled "Everybody's Ocean," wrote that it was a matter of taste whether one put on the bathing suit before coming to the beach or in the car at the beach, but that people

A large group of people pose in front of Smith's Casino, many of them wearing rented Smith's bathing suits, in January 1921. The long one-story addition was built in 1920.

had rights and attempts to force them out of the water in mid-summer would be met with vigorous resentment.

Theft continued to be a problem. There was an epidemic of the stealing of bathing suits and the thefts began to be publicized. In an interesting policy concerning gender in the year of suffrage, it was announced that bond would be $50 for men but only $25 for women. Theft continued, sometimes brazenly. In early November, one person was arrested when he went to one of the casinos boldly wearing a swimming suit taken from the casino two weeks earlier. He was convicted of larceny and paid a fine of $15. Another person went to the beach with his little daughter, who was wearing a suit owned by the casino, a suit that had been missing for two months. He was adjudged guilty and paid a $5 fine. Two weeks later, police investigated the disappearance of a patron's items from Smith's Casino. Local police said there were more slick confidence men around than at any time in the history of the beach, and urged people to keep their doors locked and allow no strangers to enter on the pretext that they were public service employees.

Groups from Miami frequently came to the casinos, especially Smith's Casino and Hardie's Casino, for daily outings at the beach throughout the summer and early fall. On October 19, for example, the American Legion had a fish chowder at Hardie's Casino. Each young man was requested to bring a young woman, either his wife, sister, or sweetheart. Hardie's was not content to wait for Miamians to come to the beach for special events. On November 6, for example, Hardie's advertised that free automobiles would be leaving from opposite the

Dan Hardie's ferry, shown in 1920, brought people from Miami to Miami Beach. Although boats were slow, the ride was scenic and faster than the crowded traffic on the causeway during busy hours.

well-known Hotel McAllister in downtown Miami every 15 minutes to bring guests to Hardie's for a dance featuring Trotter's jazz band.

In a time when Christian Sabbath observance was still relatively important, and attempts were made to make people of all religions observe it, Saturday nights were generally quiet at Miami Beach. However, on Saturday night, October 16, the "grand Atlantic ball" at Hardie's, with music by Duke Ligon and refreshments by Leon DeLeon, was a real novelty. Many young people loved to dance, so plans were made to repeat the ball the following Saturday night. With activity increasing, Hardie's also began Tuesday night dances as well as continuing Thursday-night dances. Other activities also began to increase.

Hardie's put something over on Broadway when Al Selden, a famous songwriter, sang the premier presentation of his song "On Porto Rico Isle" on October 21. He could be found at Hardie's almost any afternoon, discussing Times Square happenings with a group of fellows from Manhattan. Less than a month later, Selden announced plans to open the Sherburne Inn (formerly the Seminole Club) in Fort Dallas Park in Miami. This meant he would not regularly be at Hardie's. Claude Haddock of Miami leased a stand on "Hardie beach" to open a Coney Island refreshment booth. A few weeks later, Ben Pickering of Miami had opened a booth in Hardie's Casino for the sale of fruit drinks. He had invested $1,000 and was making refreshing drinks from real fruits right on the spot.

It was difficult to find parking space within blocks of the casinos on Sunday, October 24 when Miami Beach, according to the *Herald*, probably had the greatest number of visitors ever. Many in the crowd were Shriners, with hundreds of automobiles being seen with red-fezzed occupants. The *Miami Herald* concluded that Miami Beach was probably off to its greatest winter season ever, and that additional facilities were being built to feed and entertain the expected crowds. That same day, a local journalist reported that John A. Cook Jr., whose 5,000-room bathhouse at Coney Island was the largest on the Atlantic coast, planned to build a casino on his oceanfront lot near Fifth Street. This later would become famous as Cook's Casino.

George A. Douglass, chairman of Dade County's board of public instruction, returned from a trip to Lake City in north Florida and reported that he had met 165 cars with between two and seven passengers in each on their way to Miami. On his way back to Miami, apparently with somewhat of a heavy foot, he passed 95 cars. He reported that little towns all along the Atlantic coast were overflowing with travelers. This also led to the expectation that the Miami area was going to have its biggest season in history.

Winter rates went into effect on November 2, 1920. The opening of the Miami Beach Baths, set for the same day, was delayed indefinitely because trouble developed in the suction pipes filling the Roman pools and rough seas had prevented emergency work. By November 8, the baths were open to the public. William Jennings Bryan Jr. opened the swimming season at the beach and was the first to enter the pools. Shortly after opening the baths, Bryan declared to the Miami Real Estate Board that they could not build a city by inviting the sporting element, the dregs of society, or the underworld. He encouraged the realtors to get out the word that Miami people were interested in virtue and the higher things. One can imagine what Fisher thought of Bryan's attitude toward the sporting element, in either the literal or figurative meaning of sporting.

The short news items about Miami Beach now consisted of many listings of who was returning to Miami Beach, and Dan Hardie, owner of Hardie's Casino, received significant attention. He had been out of town for five months for rest as prescribed by his physician. He had been sheriff of Dade County from 1909 to 1917, but apparently, it was the casino that had stressed him out. He would be reelected sheriff in a landslide in 1933, but would be removed by the governor even before his first year was finished, probably because he was too tough on crime. His wife, Anna, was described as a little jewel found in the "glorious crown of womanhood."

In early November, the *Miami Herald* announced that the much-talked-about Miami Beach Club, formerly the Miami Beach Casino, was ready for membership. Generally, the winter season began with the opening of the Miami Beach Casino, but with the changing of the casino to a private club and the imminent opening of the Flamingo Hotel, the new rules were still unknown. The *Herald* highly praised the new club, saying that Miami Beach, as America's winter playground, occupied such a high place in world prestige that the club would gain the support of the many wealthy seasonal visitors and those who had winter homes in Miami Beach.

The club had "short date" memberships, including a daily visiting card for $1, and a high-class restaurant à la carte. The popular Ray Manderson Orchestra was back for another season. There also were other orchestras, including the Hoosier Sextette from Indiana. The Miami Beach Club now had jurisdiction over the beachfront at the clubhouse and baths, and J. Arthur Pancoast wanted the public to understand that the baths were still open to the public and were being run under the same system as in the previous year.

After the Miami Beach Club opened to accept memberships, but before the club actually opened, other events occurred. Armistice Day was celebrated quietly in Miami Beach, with the American Legion having a dance at the Miami Beach Club. More than 50 fifth- and sixth-graders from the Coconut Grove School spent Friday afternoon, November 19, at Smith's Casino, an award for their school grades. The only major news mention of special Thanksgiving events was the Shriners' Club of Miami's Thanksgiving eve dance and entertainment, held at Hardie's.

The following Sunday was described in the *Miami Herald*'s usual superlative language as one of the most auspicious preseason holidays in the history of Miami Beach. The newspaper noted that threatening weather did not keep thousands of pleasure-seekers from pouring into Miami Beach from early morning to late afternoon, and that casino proprietors, caught short-handed, worked feverishly to satisfy the demand for bathing suits. Reclining beach chairs made their first appearance at Smith's pavilion, and Hardie's Casino had a huge telescope erected on a tripod for people to look at ships on the ocean. The *Herald* noted that four

The Miami Beach Baths was on the southeast corner of Collins Avenue and Twenty-third Street, and faced north on Twenty-third Street. The Miami Beach Casino, changed to the Miami Beach Club, and the ocean were to the east.

boats plied between Elser Pier in downtown Miami and the beach. A long, continuous line of automobiles also creeped toward the beach, giving "the impression of a mottled sea-serpent risen from the bay and gliding with hesitant jerks over forbidden territory."

Smith's Casino continued to prepare for a booming season. Avery Smith announced that hot- and cold-water baths were to be installed, and that Adolph Pardemann would be in charge of the new features. A big 5-foot clock was being built at the pool to face the sea for swimmers in the ocean. After leasing a section of one of the new bathrooms for its members, the L.P. Club announced that many of its members were returning from the north and that it was resuming its activities with its headquarters at Smith's Casino. A new tearoom was being built on Ocean Drive near Hardie's in early December.

The opening of the Miami Beach Club on December 4 was a major event receiving much publicity. The changing of the public Miami Beach Casino into the private Miami Beach Club was a major indicator of Fisher's plans to make Miami Beach into a luxurious resort. The night before the formal opening on Friday evening, December 3, Carl and Jane Fisher hosted an intimate party for close friends at the club, including Princess Camporeale (her name was also spelled Camporiale, Comporele, and Canposale) of Palermo, Italy. The small gathering included a total of 85 guests, "just the right number for a gay private function."

This photo of the Miami Beach Casino was taken February 22, 1920 by Claude Matlack. Matlock was famous as a local photographer and opened a studio at the Miami Beach Baths.

In preparation for the season, Hardie's Casino had built a high fence along the south to cut off the view of objectionable structures and the casino had been redecorated and painted in light blue and white. While Fisher was oriented to the wealthy visitors, Hardie and Smith were improving their facilities for visitors from both the Miami area and distant places.

Hardie's Casino was now the location of the West Indies Importing Company, with unique work that involved coloring being placed on photographic prints with the aid of a toothpick and a tuft of cotton. Meanwhile, Regello Duran, lessee of the dining room at Smith's Casino, had opened a beach lunchroom in one of the beach houses to sell sandwiches and fruit from baskets to bathers. He also was opening a cabaret in the dance hall at the casino with a five-piece orchestra.

Claude Matlack, locally famous as a photographer, opened a Miami Beach branch of his photographic studio at his former headquarters in the Miami Beach Baths. There were pictures of local people, beautiful homes, and bathing beauties. While Matlack would become known primarily as Carl Fisher's photographer, he was busy taking many photographs around the area.

At the Miami Beach Club, the opening night was well attended and was described as a brilliant dinner and dance, with predictions that the club would be the center of social life for the winter. The *Miami Metropolis* noted that the club was going to be a rendezvous for the younger set and their elders.

On Monday night, December 6, the Advertising Club held a banquet and dance at the Miami Beach Club, the third social event in four days. Known as the "Annual Round-Up of the Truth Crusaders," the banquet included a program of six complete vaudeville acts and several other features. Mayor T.E. James of Miami Beach and Mayor William Pruden Smith of Miami both spoke. A highlight of the evening was when newsboys broke into the crowd shouting "Extra, Extra *Metropolis*." They distributed a special comical edition of the *Miami Metropolis* announcing Miami's capture of Atlanta by the ad men. Among the approximately 117 guests were Mr. and Mrs. Carl Fisher, Mr. and Mrs. B.B. Tatum, and Mrs. Marjory Stoneman Douglas.

The Miami Beach Club also provided services to guests. For example, Filipino wares were on exhibition with demonstrations available. Handbags of bamboo with black-and-white designs and hemp handles, made by schoolchildren in the Philippines, were popular, but the hemp and bamboo hats were the latest rage. The women found them both sun- and weather-proof, and convenient for both dress and sport wear. Men could pick numerous novelties from all over the world.

While Miami Beach's "society" was meeting at the private Miami Beach Club, a sub-headline in the *Miami Metropolis* noted that "Enormous Crowds Thronged the Bathing Beaches, Dipped in the Pools, and Took Airplane Flights." The casinos again had their "biggest day of the season" (according to the local newspapers, a record that was broken frequently) on Sunday, December 5. The *Metropolis* noted the following:

> Every lunch room owner, novelty booth proprietor, souvenir dealer, and peanut merchant at the south end carried Sunday's receipts away in sacks . . . New eating places did a "standing room only" business . . . Both casinos sold out of bathing suits before late afternoon and the late comers were compelled to sit in the sand and watch more fortunate and earlier arriving folks dashing about in the waves . . . During the afternoon a big hydroplane called at the beach and began taking up passengers for $5 Flights.[5]

The article also noted that a cashing stand had been built at the Miami Beach Baths and that, for the first time this season, nonmembers had to pay for admission to the beach. Smith's Casino soon would have another electric pump installed to double the capacity for filling its swimming pool. The Miami Beach Baths was still getting most of its business in the afternoon, with the "noon" hours from 11 a.m. until 2 p.m. still slow. They expected the noon hours to be the busiest by January 1, 1921.

Hardie's Casino leased a concession for the manufacture of Saratoga chips and candy apples, wholesale and retail. A 14-foot by 24-foot stand was being built on the Zapf property on Ocean Drive to manufacture saltwater taffy and root beer for retail. Mr. Stanton, owner of the Bungalow Restaurant on Ocean Drive, had organized a Limerick Club. Prizes for giving a missing line to verse were doughnuts (the common spelling then for today's donuts), for which Stanton's was famous. Stanton also was also known for the unsuccessful drive to change the name of Miami Beach to "Miami-by-the-Sea."

The casino area in South Beach was the site of a special entertainment, on December 9, by Andre de Monceaux, who had resigned as city policeman a few days earlier because of questions about a jailbreak, and Tony Muto, the new lifeguard at Hardie's Casino. The *Miami Metropolis* referred to de Monceaux as a French soldier of fortune, wearer of the Victory medal, ex-police officer, ex-racing automobile driver, and ex-Mexican adventurer. He claimed to represent the clan of Haig & Haig of the loyal order of Scotch Highballers and was ready to dance to the shrill note of the pibroch. Anthony "Tony" Muto had been around the world twice, claiming to have baked in the straits of Singapore, frozen in Afghanistan, beach combed at Bombay, herded sheep in New Zealand, and passed coal on all seven seas. He had hitchhiked to Miami Beach from Narragansett at a cost of $20, and reported that his little notebook was filled with names of fellows who had given him a lift and a meal. People around Hardie's Casino considered Muto a character and beloved vagabond, and included him in all the good times. On this particular day, he was impersonating a hula-hula queen and claiming to belong to local union # 492 of shimmy dancers. The *Miami Metropolis* noted that Tony did the shimmy and Andre essayed the sworddance and that, for hours, the merry pair kept the South Beach folks in an uproar. It was not the type of entertainment one found at the Miami Beach Club, but it was very enjoyable.

As part of the first annual Palm Fete celebration, Miami Beach entered a float in the Flower Parade in Miami and won first prize in the community float class with Neptune and the figure of Venus rising out of the sea. Palm Fete was a week-long celebration. Most of the events took place in Miami, but there was one day of major festivities at Miami Beach. On Friday, December 10, the events were centered around the Miami Beach Baths and the surrounding area. The *Miami Daily Metropolis*, claiming that Miami was greatly depopulated due to the beach's celebration for the festival, especially for the bathing suit parade, reported that such a crowd had never been seen in Miami Beach. The newspaper said that the most beautiful girls on the east coast were exhibiting the season's latest bathing suits and that every spectator had a good view because of the long parade.

The bathing suit parade was the highlight of the day, marching from the Miami Beach Baths north to J. Arthur Pancoast's house, and back to the baths. There were more than 1,000 cars parked around Twenty-second and Twenty-third Streets before noon, waiting for the parade, and about 5,000 cars in the area. The bathing suits were either in the silk suit class or the knit wool suit class, and contestants were in either the "Stouts, Annette Kellermans, or Flappers" categories. There were no age limits. Pose and poise were also considered. Ralph Kuffner of the Miami Beach wireless station won third prize in the humorous costumes category. Kuffner was the only man in the parade, and he wore a barrel that carried a label saying "Who stole my suit?" J. Arthur Pancoast, manager of the

These pictures show the bathing suit parade at the first annual Palm Fete (Fest) in Miami Beach in 1920. Note that some women are wearing bathing suits from different time periods.

Miami Beach Baths, announced that he planned to show "The Evolution of the Bathing Suit" in the parade, with women wearing costumes from 1890, 1900, 1910, and 1920. He claimed that the 1920 one-piece bathing suit would cause a riot on any northern beach, but that it was only for parade purposes.

The bathing suit parade renewed the controversy over women's bathing suits, an issue that would not go away. The *Miami Herald* said that the reformers would have shuddered if they had seen the parade. The *Miami Metropolis* also wrote in support of the new bathing suits. The day also included a number of aquatic events: various length dashes, races, and relays, diving competitions, and life saving exhibitions. The Miami Beach Club was dolled up, kept open house all day, and had many luncheon parties. Hardie's Casino held moon dances nightly during Palm Fete week.

The controversy over bathing suits continued on a national level in 1920, with a major involvement from the Women's Christian Temperance Union (WCTU). Nationally, the WCTU advocated the covering of nude statues and opposed ballet because of the pink tights worn by ballerinas. Some allies even supported the covering of nude piano legs. Most attention was given to women's bathing suits in 1920, but there were also some people who were advocating a new "topless" bathing suit for men. In 1920, men's bathing suits usually were one piece and covered the chest. Despite some local and national traditionalists, Miami Beach generally maintained a progressive attitude on bathing suits and related topics. After all, Miami Beach was a playground.

The Miami Beach Casino was on the Atlantic Ocean, with a beautiful beach. The one-piece bathing suit, covering the chest, was still popular with men as well as women.

At night, after the controversial bathing suit parade, there was a parade of decorated yachts with parties next to the causeway. Of course, there were some problems. One boat went aground and began leaking south of the causeway, and three trips by sailors were necessary to save the passengers. Another boat became stranded on the side of the channel while being turned to get in position in line at the Miami Beach Electric Company plant. The passengers, including R.E. Hall, Dade County's superintendent of public instruction, were not able to get off the boat until almost midnight.

A few days later, operation of some of the "entertainment" wheels in booths in South Beach became so obviously involved in gambling that the city marshal stopped all of them on Monday. At one wheel, there was open gambling for money all day Sunday. The police commissioner said that flagrant and open money games had been going on in South Beach for several weeks, and that the operations would be closed down if they did not stop.

On December 15, the Miami Beach Club celebrated the formal opening of its balcony, as well as the premier performance of its new orchestra, the much heralded Hoosier Sextet. The club continued to have weekly Saturday night dinner dances. At the dance on December 18, many joked, at the post office's expense, regarding a number of invitations that had been mailed in Miami sometime before the club's opening of December 4 but had been delivered two weeks after the opening.

On December 16, Dan Hardie leased out 150 feet of land facing Ocean Drive near his casino to the Ben Krause Carnival company. The carnival company planned to open as soon as electric power could be supplied and would include a 60-foot Ferris wheel, an 80-foot whip, and a merry-go-round. The Ferris wheel was the largest portable Ferris wheel ever built, the whip was a $12,000 ride made famous at Coney Island, and the carousel cost $10,000 and had a real band organ. The carnival opened on December 19, one day later than scheduled. The Ben Krause Carnival received high praise, with people saying that the employees were well behaved and courteous, that there were no questionable concessions attached to the carnival, and that the company was better than others. Meanwhile, it was reiterated by the Miami Beach police commissioner that gambling would not be allowed at the wheels and that they would be allowed to continue only if participants behaved well.

Dan Hardie also hired Captain Jack Williams as the swimming instructor at the casino for the season. The 85-year-old Williams had the distinction of being the oldest swimming instructor in the world, had saved 62 lives, and was a world champion swimmer. Hardie was also visited by his friend Joseph Fralinger of Atlantic City, one of the first people to build a boardwalk and manufacture saltwater taffy in Atlantic City, and the person who had earlier encouraged a boardwalk for South Beach. Fred Roberts of Miami was making plans to open a lunch stand in Hardie's building in the space at the rear of the pool.

Dan Hardie was a busy man. He transplanted three large coconut palms from his Ocean Drive property to the beach in front of his casino. The newspaper noted that the palms gave a real touch of the tropics to the beach and were a notable spot for the snapshot feature of bathing.

On Monday, December 20, the Miami Beach Baths took on the real "winter season" atmosphere for the first time. Many winter tourists were at the baths, with the main attraction being two little sisters, ages four and six, who could swim "like ducks." The Freckles Club, which required that its members have freckles, "although only a very few could make one eligible," met at the Miami Beach Baths. The club had been organized by Bob Steele "just for fun," and had a large following of children who listened to marvelous American fairy stories (most of them original) by Mr. Steele.

The casinos lost big on Saturday and Sunday, December 18 and 19, because the beaches were edged with crude oil and the surface of the water was covered with the slick stuff. Oil ships had caused spills by blowing out their bilges by steam. Hundreds of people did not go into the water and actually tore up the casinos' bath towels to wash tar off their feet. Dan Hardie said he did not think the oil spill was intentional, but merely thoughtless. There was talk of petitioning the city council to try to stop the practice. Earlier, a yacht owner had complained about oil floating in the ocean in front of Miami Beach and accumulating along the shores enough to interfere with bathing. It was thought that these oil "strikes" occurred periodically because large boats in the Gulf Stream were cleaning their engines, and there was little or no governmental regulation of the ships. On December 15, Avery Smith appeared before the city council to tell about the very inadequate toilet facilities in the south end of the city.

On Thursday, only two days before Christmas, with the half-holiday still being observed, both Hardie's Casino and Smith's Casino had their busiest weekday of the season. The south end of Miami Beach was "a miniature Coney Island." Christmas day consisted mostly of private parties at home, but the Miami Beach Club was decorated with trees, flowers, and tinsel hangings, and had several lunch and dancing parties. The biggest Christmas event in Miami Beach was the Christmas Eve party given for children at the indoor tennis courts on Lincoln Road by Mrs. Carl Fisher.

The Miami Beach Baths added a graduate physiotherapist and a barber, G. Valentin, who had the distinction of having cut the hair of at least two of the royal heads of Europe: King Edward VII of England and King George V of England (while he was still a prince).

Smith's Casino was the site of the L.P. Club's semi-annual election of officers the day after Christmas. Elected unanimously as officers were the following: L.P. Fuchs, president; L.P. Pryor, vice president; L.P. Campbell, financial secretary; L.P. Kroshel, recording secretary; and L.P. Trautman, sport master. Obviously, "L.P." were popular initials. Famous for their rough, playful fun, the L.P. Club then put their initiates through a stunt where the candidate for initiation was blind-folded and mounted on a bike headed toward Bimini. Something always happened to the unsinkable mechanism of the machine and the candidate was rudely dumped into the ocean.

Gertrude Bennett and Joseph Hess, "a clever dancing team," were at the Miami Beach Club in late December to perform. They gave their first performance on Christmas night and made nightly appearances at the club after that time. They also provided instructions in advanced ballroom dancing every afternoon for members only in the club balcony. A phonograph had been installed, "kindly lent by Ye Music Shop of Miami." A children's class, to meet two afternoons a week, was being organized to teach calisthenics and dancing. The Pan-Hellenic Society had a formal banquet and dance at the Miami Beach Club on December 29. The private Miami Beach Club ended 1920 and began 1921 with a spectacular formal New Year's Eve dinner and dance on December 31. Fronds decorated each column and arch along the main floor and balcony, and brightly colored balloons adorned the chairs along with make-believe birds and alligators. Poinsettias and bougainvillea, furnished by Mrs. Carl Fisher, added splashes of natural color to the club. On December 31, 1920, Roy Mack, the Miami Beach Club's manager, wrote to Fisher that the club membership was rapidly reaching the 500 mark, saying that Fisher should encourage his friends to get their applications in as soon as possible because the club might not be able to take any more season members after reaching that number. So ended 1920 at the former Miami Beach Casino, now the newly reorganized, private, and very successful Miami Beach Club.

As the examples mentioned in this chapter show, social life at Hardie's Casino, Smith's Casino, the Miami Beach Casino, which became the Miami Beach Club, and the Miami Beach Baths had been fantastic during 1920. The good times, with the addition of the Flamingo Hotel, would increase even more in the future.

The swimming pool at Smith's Casino was popular with all ages. In addition to a pool on the Atlantic Ocean, Smith's Casino also had a playground for children.

7. The Sporting Life

A polo match was recorded as early as 600 B.C., but by the 1800s, it survived only in a few areas of India. Polo was introduced into the United States in 1875, but it was confined mostly to the East Coast, where it was a pastime for the wealthy class. Starting in 1919 and lasting until 1939, the United States became the leading polo country, with the sport still limited to the wealthy. The elitism of polo playing fit perfectly into Carl Fisher's dreams for Miami Beach.

Carl Fisher introduced polo to Miami Beach in 1919, the first polo game ever played in Florida being played at Fisher's Miami Beach polo fields in February 1919. By 1920, its second season, polo was already very popular in Miami Beach, partly because it was popular among the fashionable set and partly because of Fisher's personal strong support. He loved fast sports and he recognized the appeal of polo to the type of people he wanted to attract to Miami Beach. Among those who played in Miami Beach were Rodney Wanamaker (he also played a major role in golf, but not in Miami Beach) and Julius Fleischmann. Fisher's polo field went from Meridian Avenue to Lenox Avenue, and from shortly south of Lincoln Road to Fifteenth Street (north of today's Flamingo Park). The clubhouse was just south of Lincoln Road between Jefferson Avenue and Michigan Avenue.

On January 2, 1920, the *Miami Metropolis* announced on its front page that the first polo match of the season would be on January 15. Upward of 100 polo ponies were already guaranteed on the field and were being exercised daily. Although in excellent condition, the polo field was still being worked on to make it even better. Polo was to be featured as the one great sport at Miami Beach in 1920 and it was expected to be popular with the public. A season membership without a parking space was $20, while daily admittance was $1 for non-members. Children under 14 were admitted for half price. Season parking spaces were an expensive $100, $60, or $40, with occupants of the cars free. Daily parking spaces were $5 per car, with all occupants free.

The *Miami Herald* reported on January 4 that 12 polo ponies had arrived the previous evening. Additional polo ponies continued to arrive, and some of them were safely housed in the new and up-to-date stables that had recently been built near the polo fields. By January 6, polo practice was in full swing at the Miami Beach polo field, and the first real practice polo game in the season took place on

This polo match shows the viewing stands in the background, just south of Lincoln Road.
The clubhouse was between Jefferson Avenue and Lenox Avenue on the northern edge of
the grounds.

January 9. The *Miami Herald* wrote that Miami Beach had one of the best polo
fields in the South, and that polo at Miami Beach was expected to be one of the
society events of the Southern season. Outstanding saddle horses had been
brought for sale or hire and the Miami Beach Polo Club was planning to sponsor
a big horse show. A grand polo pony parade to show the public the kind of stock
was announced and acclaimed an immense success. The *Miami Herald* stated
that, by the time the north had thawed and the tourists had returned to their
homes, the polo history of Miami Beach would have been written prominently in
1920 records.

Polo practice went on every evening and the first big game of the season was
played between the Miami Beach Polo Club and a team from Palm Beach on
January 27. Contestants and about 70 ponies paraded before the match, the 200-
space parking lot was basically filled, and Miami Beach won 8 to 3.5. Aside from
the sporting importance, the social prestige was illustrated in a headline entitled
"First Polo Game of Season Is Event in Brilliant Social Life." The article named
about 150 people attending the match and concluded that the many gay parties
associated with polo indicated that society would focus its interest on the new
polo field.

Two days later, Miami Beach and Palm Beach played again, with Palm Beach
winning this time. On Tuesdays, Thursdays, and Saturdays, with Thursday being

the main day, polo games continued with the newspapers noting weather conditions in relation to games and the arrival of new players. Driving south to Florida was still a problem because roads frequently washed out somewhere along the hundreds of miles, and a few players were too tired to play because of their fatigue from the trip.

Julius Fleischmann, the famous yeast manufacturer from Cincinnati, arrived with his family on February 5. The paper noted that all of Fleischmann's ponies were veterans, unlike a majority of other ponies. Two of his ponies were named Yeastman and Yeast Care. The new Mrs. Julius Fleischmann was perhaps the most interesting figure on the polo grounds, and was often pointed out. Interestingly, Julius Fleischmann could play polo with Fisher, but could not enter Fisher's clubhouse when it later opened because of Fisher's anti-Jewish restrictions.

A *Miami Metropolis* article entitled "Polo Charms Sportsmen and Society Folks Alike" stated that no other counter-attractions could claim real sports lovers. While part of the attraction of polo was social, there was also an emphasis on the sporting aspect. The *Metropolis* wrote that good games, like one recently played, gave people a taste of the real thing and that nothing else would content them. One unidentified observing visitor wrote that women adored polo, but that the male visitors to Miami Beach said it reminded them of tiddledewinks [*sic*] on horseback. Tickets cost $5.

This photo shows Jane Fisher on the left and her mother-in-law Ida Graham Fisher on the right. The beauty of palm trees was another major advertisement for Miami Beach.

Fisher was an avid sportsman who liked to play polo, although apparently not very well if we believe one spectator's letter. The unidentified observing visitor wrote that he admired Fisher as the angel of Miami Beach, but not as a polo player. In his opinion, Fisher had almost fallen off his horse several times. The visitor wrote that he would have himself tied on the horse and take Fisher's place if necessary. Another letter, perhaps from the same individual, but published in another column about a month later, said that polo was supposed to be very exciting, but that many people were yawning during the game. This letter also said that one player, who was 40 years old and fat, looked like he might slip off the horse, suggesting that the two letters were written by the same individual. Carl Fisher, born January 12, 1874, was 46 years old. Jane Fisher, Carl's wife, had a different perception of her husband's polo abilities. She wrote that Carl rode a horse for the first time in his late 40s when he decided to play polo, and that his trained cyclist's body reacted as if he had been born to the saddle.

A special event, the Grand Gymkhana, under the auspices of the Miami Beach Polo Club, was held on March 3, with many people attending. Gymkhana, a Hindu word for "field day," originated among British cavalrymen in India and came from England to the United States. Although the correct spelling is "gymkhana," both Miami newspapers spelled it "gymkana." The Gymkhana consisted of flat races of about 4 furlongs, a hurdle race over six flights of hurdles, musical chairs on ponies, a "bending race," where contestants raced around posts 50 yards apart, a costume race, and a grapefruit race. In musical chairs, the riders circled the chairs on their ponies and, at the sound of a whistle, dismounted and sought a chair while still holding the pony bridle. In the costume race, the contestant had to race to a point, dismount, light a cigar, put on a costume, raise a parasol, remount, and race back to the starting point. In the grapefruit race, contestants had to put grapefruits in a bucket using a spear, while contestants tried to obstruct and interfere with each other. The first person to put six grapefruits in a bucket was the winner. Gymkhana day was also a special day for children, and many families brought their youngsters. Women also took part in the games; three of the riders rode sidesaddle. The newspaper reported, however, that those who rode astride (straddling the horse) won the prizes.

The polo season was short, running from mid-January to mid-March. There had been previous correspondence between Fisher and the Cuban polo team and on Tuesday, March 9, the newspaper announced that the games that week would probably be the last of the season. The Thursday and Saturday games would be the first ever played between the United States and Cuban teams. The winner of the Tuesday game would be the team to play against the Cuban team, with the four United States players being Bob Hassler, Jesse Andrew, Julius Fleischmann, and Harold E. Talbot.

A Cuban group was registered at the Breakers Hotel; its team consisted of Captain J. Adlaberto Gimenez, aide-de-camp of the president of Cuba (Mario Garcia Menocal); Colonel Eugenio Silva, commandant of the Cuban army (Camp Columbia); Captain R. Salmon; and Commandant Luis Beltran. On

Wednesday, Carl Fisher, Julius Fleischmann, and a few others entertained all the members of the Cuban polo team at a luncheon at the Miami Beach Casino.

The match between the United States and Cuban teams on Thursday, March 11, the first international contest ever played between a Cuba and a United States team, was described as the greatest day in the history of Miami Beach. The *Miami Herald*, again in flowery prose, described the gathering as the largest, the most fashionable, and the most brilliant ever assembled in Miami Beach. Every parking space was taken, hundreds of spectators were on foot, the members' enclosure was packed to excess, and the day was ideal in every way. The United States team won 6 to 5, but the Cuban players and their followers showed wild enthusiasm in cheering for the winners.

At the end of the match, the two polo teams and their friends were entertained with refreshments, music, dancing, and socializing. The site for the celebration was the impressive yacht of Mrs. Julius Fleischmann. Then, a large ball in honor of the Cuban team and the visitors was held at the Miami Beach Casino. All Cuban visitors were invited to take flights in the Curtiss planes and, on Saturday, the second game was played. The newspaper reported that the Cuban army officers and prominent Cuban gentry in Miami Beach with the team made the game the most notable of the season. Mario Menocal Jr., the son of Cuba's president, was present, as well as the pretty Russian princess Xenia De Waldeck. With attention to fashion detail, particularly for prominent people, the *Miami Herald* reported that the princess was wearing a gown of rose crepe with a matching hat. The United States team won again, and thus won the international cup.

On Monday, the Cubans and Americans gave a free exhibition game, which the Cuban team won, but this game almost ended in a serious misunderstanding between the Cuban and Miami Beach teams. The Miami Beach team convinced the Cuban team to play two extra periods, but the Miami Beach team leader had the last period extended to 17 minutes instead of 10. The Miami Beach team played tough, attempting, in Carl Fisher's words, "to beat hell-out-of-them and beating on a terrible overtime period." Fisher apologized to the Cuban team and fired his Miami Beach team leader with a strongly worded criticism.

Jane Fisher hosted a party at their home, The Shadows, for the Cuban team after the end of the games. Jane and Carl also presented a magnificent horse named Miami Boy to Colonel Silva. Colonel Silva spoke, assuring them that his memory of them and their hospitality, and the wonders of Miami Beach, would live with him forever.

On Monday night, March 15, the Cuban visitors entertained their hosts with a dance at the Miami Beach Casino. In a speech, ex-mayor J. Bookwalter of Indianapolis assured Colonel Silva and his associates of the following:

> The bonds of friendship which were created in the dark days of the
> period of your country, those bonds which bind the people of America
> to the people of Cuba, have only been cemented more firmly and

strongly by your coming here on this occasion. This is only the forerunner of many similar events . . . and in the years which will come we trust that the opportunity to meet you will be presented to us once more at least.[1]

The dance ended the polo season activity for 1920. Colonel Silva expressed support for steamship communication between Havana and Miami and, on March 27, the *Miami Herald* announced that Señor Miguel Caballero, the first Cuban consul ever assigned to Miami, had opened offices in Miami and would look after the increasing trade between the United States and Cuba. The newspaper also noted that Señor Caballero's two granddaughters had entered St. Catherine's Academy in Miami as students.

The polo season ended and, two weeks later, the newspapers reported the end of the season by writing that J.C. Andrew and his polo ponies had gone back to Indianapolis, and that only Fisher had done more than Andrew for local polo. Fisher and Andrew jointly owned at least 20 high-class polo ponies, including several of the best in the country. On April 12, Fisher wrote that he had received a long letter from Colonel Silva describing the building of polo grounds and the great enthusiasm in Havana. Silva hoped that in 1921 there would be international polo games and tournaments in Cuba, as well as tennis, golf, Jack-a-lay, basketball, and swimming.

This photo, taken March 11, 1920, shows a group of Cuban officials who were in Miami Beach for the polo match between the Cuban team and the Miami Beach team.

Cuban officials, in Miami Beach for the polo matches, are shown in this photo taken on February 26, 1920.

There was almost no interest in polo during the summer, but near the end of September, the *Miami Metropolis* noted that Fisher was negotiating to bring some of the fastest northern polo teams to Miami Beach for the winter games. Fisher was so optimistic about the upcoming polo season that he had already begun building a new practice field between Drexel Avenue and Meridian Avenue. The new field was to be 850 feet long by 430 feet wide, a little smaller than a regular field. A regular polo field is 900 feet long and 480 feet wide. An expert in Bermuda grass was working to get grass on the new field.

Plans were being made to play games in Miami Beach with a team from London and it was expected that some of the nationally known United States polo players in Miami Beach would represent the country in England in the summer of 1921 in an attempt to regain the International Challenge Cup. The United States government recently had added polo as part of military training in colleges and universities, and this was expected to greatly increase interest in polo and to lead to collegiate fours being played in Miami Beach.

The physical beauty of Fisher's polo field in Miami Beach was also discussed in detail in the *Miami Daily Metropolis*:

> Livestock's aid to the picturesque setting of the polo fields will be flocks
> of sheep cropping the grass on the green acres. This charming, restful

rural effect can be pictured in the mind. The green hedges, such as mark the boundaries of English farms, being used for controls, the flocks of pure white sheep brousing [*sic*], the shepherd and the collie dog attending the flocks, all this such a picture as few nooks and corners of America can give with more charm and beauty.[2]

On October 12, Fisher received a note from Len Warner of the *Miami Daily Metropolis* staff, with copies of local and editorial references to subjects in which Fisher had recently expressed an interest. Warner told Fisher to send whatever timely suggestions occurred to him, and that he (Warner) would do the best he could with them. Fisher assiduously courted the local newspapers, especially in a time when some newspapers extensively printed prewritten articles submitted to them. A week later, Fisher thanked Warner for his editorials and said that he was reading so many flattering statements that he was beginning to believe them himself. On October 9, the *Miami Daily Metropolis* published a special Flamingo Hotel Section that was very positive about Miami Beach. On the same day, there was an editorial that praised Miami Beach, saying that the earlier vision was developing into "magnificent consummation" under the "mastermind" of Fisher. Fisher also told Warner that he was planning the biggest polo season ever, but that the names of the players he was lining up should not be published until December because it would cause a lot of hard feelings if published sooner.

Fisher was not the only person building more structures for polo. Harold Talbot of Dayton, Ohio, a winter resident of Miami Beach and "one of the most successful players that figured in last season's polo at the beach," had erected barns near his new home at the northwest corner of Tenth Street and West Avenue. He was in town for a few days to make arrangements for at least 24 high-grade ponies. In the 1919 season, Talbot had the largest number of ponies in Miami Beach.

After spending four months in Indianapolis, Fisher returned to Miami Beach on November 4. Polo fever was rising and, on November 6, the *Metropolis* reported that ponies would be shipped from northern stables to Miami Beach at intervals over the next eight weeks. The newspaper also reported that Miami Beach was competing in polo with the big California resorts and that Miami Beach had beat them by signing up some of the best men in the polo world to play at Miami Beach. Polo was also going strong in Cuba. The *Metropolis* reported that a Cuban team would be sent to Miami Beach and that a Miami Beach team would probably go to Cuba during the coming winter.

Dormitories and mess halls were being built to house and feed 60 trainers and, on November 18, 1920, Fisher and L.A. Young opened the season's practice with the comment that Miami Beach had the fastest polo turf in the country.

Fisher continued his efforts to bring the best names in sports to Miami Beach to help develop the reputation of the oceanfront community as a place for the wealthy. On December 1, 1920, the *Miami Metropolis* announced that Jimmy Cooley of Meadowbrook would shortly be in Miami Beach, that he was a real live polo wire, that he wrote for *Spur* and *Town & Country*, that there would be unlimited polo news, and that Cooley made the game big wherever he was. Fisher was determined to make Miami Beach a top polo city and money was no problem. In polo, as in golf, tennis, and boat racing, he brought big names to Miami Beach.

George Miller from Austin, Texas, who was described as the keenest polo pony breeder in the United States, brought 20 "cream of trained" polo ponies to Miami Beach in December. He said that Miami Beach was the best place in the world to play polo, even better than southern California where there was too much rain. The arrival of prominent owners of polo ponies, of famous players, and of outstanding ponies continued almost daily. On December 20, holders of parking spaces from the previous season were urged to reserve their spaces before January 1. After then, it would be first come, first served and "Incoming persons who are polo fans and fanatics will be clamoring for the places." There were only 400 parking spaces on the first line about the fields and some games would bring 2,000 cars, so that cars would be parked four or five deep.

On Saturday, December 18, Carl Fisher, George Miller, and F.C. Andrews were defeated in the first polo game of the season, but the game was only a practice tryout. Work was soon begun on more stables, a "stable famine" having developed because of the number of ponies. Local papers reported on December 21 that Jimmy Cooley had arrived in town, and that real earnest polo practice would begin immediately. Cooley, who had managed more big polo events than any American and who was referred to as the "polo dictator" at Miami Beach, named many prominent owners he expected in Miami Beach for the polo season soon unless the stock market situation became too negative.

During the last week of December 1920, the Tuesday-Thursday-Saturday schedule was changed to Monday-Wednesday-Saturday because many of the men in Miami Beach were making a big trip to Havana starting Wednesday evening. The *Miami Metropolis*, supporting Cooley's concern, also announced that some of the polo men would be arriving in Miami Beach about two weeks late because the New York stock market and first of the year financing was delaying their departure. But the groundwork had been laid and Miami Beach ended 1920 with great plans for polo in 1921.

Along with polo, golf was the major outdoor activity in Miami Beach in 1920, and these two would receive much more attention than other outdoor sports. Golf had the advantage of having a much longer playing season than polo, and it was available to a greater number of potential players. Golf did not have as much prestige as polo, but it had enough to fit into Fisher's vision for Miami Beach. Golf, largely as we know it today, was developed in Scotland by the 1400s. In 1786, a golf club was started in Charleston, South Carolina, but the game did not catch on in the United States until the 1880s. Golf continued to be an elitist sport in Europe and many professionals from Scotland and England came to the United States as golf teachers. United States professional tours began in 1922, often sponsored by wealthy individuals in resort areas to promote real estate. Of course, this also had an influence on Fisher. By the 1920s, the United States was beginning to be the international leader in golf.

The Miami Beach Historical Association encourages education and research on the city's social history. Pictured here are the board of directors, Mayor David Dermer, and City Commissioner Matti Herrera Bower. From left to right are Bower, Anthony T.P. Brooks, Dr. Abe Lavender (board president), Dermer, Dr. Judith Berson-Levinson, board member and city commissioner Luis R. Garcia Jr., and Carolyn Klepser. Not shown is board member Stuart Reed, Esq.

The course for the Miami Beach Golf and Country Club was on the north side of Lincoln Road, across from the Lincoln Hotel. The course had 18 holes, 10 on the south side between Lincoln Road and the Collins Canal, and 8 on the north side of the Collins Canal going to West Twenty-eighth Street. On the south side of Collins Canal, the golf course went from Miami (Washington) Avenue, which as late as 1918 was known as Golf Course Drive (north of Lincoln Road), to the bridle path about two-thirds of a block east of Meridian Avenue. On the north side of the canal, the course went from Pine Tree Drive to Prairie Avenue. The clubhouse was located on the south side of Collins Canal and is one of the few 1920 buildings remaining in Miami Beach.

An article on January 4 noted that the increasing interest in golf was causing the Miami Beach golf links to be alive with golfers from all over the country. The article gave visitors names and states, which included eight people from New York, five from Pennsylvania, three from Minnesota, three from Ohio, two from Michigan, two from Illinois, one from New Jersey, one from Indiana, and one each from Miami and Tampa. Golf reports were regular features in the news, ranging from weather conditions to tournament play and their reception in the community. Community leaders and local journalists expected golf to be quite popular throughout the tourist season and believed that the sport would have special events about every week, including activities for junior players.

A number of professionals made Miami Beach their winter home. The Miami Beach Golf and Country Club had a tournament of one type or another every week, mixed foursomes were enjoyed, and golfers continued to be mentioned by name in the newspaper. The recognition was part of the social attraction of Miami Beach. The names also suggested the geographical diversity and cosmopolitanism of Miami Beach visitors.

Almost daily reports continued and, on February 4, Willie Park, considered the best-known golf architect in the country, arrived to lay out the new 18-hole golf course on what was referred to as the fill on the north side of Collins Canal across from a group of clubhouses. Mike Brady of Boston, considered perhaps the best golfer in the country, had played in Miami Beach the day before and liked it. As with polo, golf combined sporting and social life. Afternoon tea was described as

> becoming quite the thing served on the veranda of the club tea room overlooking the canal. The luncheon hour is quite the thing too and motorists are finding it convenient to drop in for either luncheon or tea, even if they do not care to play golf.[3]

Although the polo season ended in mid-March, the Miami Beach Golf and Country Club continued to be popular with no sign that the season was nearing an end. Near the end of March, golfers stopped playing long enough one day to enjoy tea and the novelty of having their pictures taken in connection with the visit of Olive Thomas and other leading members of the Selznick Pictures Corporation, who were in town filming scenes for *The Flapper*. Only a few golf bugs were playing daily and many golfers were going farther up the state to escape the warming weather. The club remained open until June, although the

The Miami Beach Golf and Country Club, on the Collins Canal, was also mistakenly identified by this postcard as being located in Miami.

clubhouse would be closed, and Miami members helped to keep the course open for playing all summer.

At the beginning of April, Fisher announced that he would stay in Miami Beach during part of the summer instead of going to Indianapolis, but that the Miami Beach Casino, the Lincoln Hotel, the golf clubhouse, and some other places would be closed. Fisher went to Indianapolis for about six or seven weeks, but by July 3, he had returned to Miami Beach.

On April 13, the Miami Beach Golf and Country Club suffered greatly when the new locker house, a one-story structure with 300 steel lockers, caught fire, resulting in a total loss of the inside of the building and the contents. The fire had burned during the night unnoticed and only the concrete walls remained. The lockers had been the latest addition to the club's equipment, after a delay of almost eight months due to shipping problems and, once the lockers were installed, the locker house had been the pride of the golfers. The cause of the fire was unknown and there was no insurance. When Carl Fisher was asked what he was going to do about it, he replied in two words: "Build another."

Despite the fire, golfing continued and, at the end of April, plans were again discussed for a new golf course, the Miami Beach Bay Shore course. Lee Nelson, a professional golfer, was to lay out the new course, which was to be as "sporty" as any in Florida. Acknowledging that the new course was still mostly on paper, a local writer noted that the Miami Beach golf course would be left to beginners and that the new Bay Shore course, with its extensive fairways and its difficult approach shots, would be for experts. The new course would be much more elaborate than the current course. Willie Park had been paid $2,000 for drawing the blueprints.

A little later, the *Metropolis* published elaborate plans for the Miami Beach Bay Shore Golf and Country Club House, noting that it was to be an imposing building of hollow tile with stucco finish. The clubhouse would face the dredged Sunset Lake and the deep waterway would allow some boats to tie up before the country club. With four open-air balconies, a dining room seating 100, a locker room with 400 lockers, plus lounges, offices, and other facilities, the building was expected to cost $60,000.

The locker house that had burned in April at the Miami Beach Golf and Country Club was rebuilt by early June. The Bay Shore course was still under construction and a new course was also being worked on near the Flamingo Hotel, which was being built at the same time with an end-of-the-year opening planned. Meanwhile, Lee Nelson was scanning the sky every day for the rain clouds necessary for the grass and complaining that if he didn't want rain, it would be raining.

Little attention was given to golf over the summer by the local papers, which said that "no one" was playing at the Miami Beach course in June. The *Miami Metropolis*'s "Beach Brevities" said that golfers were playing up north where the sun was hotter at midday than it was in Miami Beach, but that there was no reason why there shouldn't be as much golf in June as in November in Miami Beach.

The local newspapers frequently listed visitors playing on the golf course. On January 16, 1920, for example, golfers included Mr. and Mrs. C.D. Dallas of Winnetka, Illinois; W.F.D. Daniels and H.G. Lavinder of Bristol, Virginia; and W.E. Phillips of Boston, Massachusetts, illustrating the usual geographical diversity.

With October and the preparation for the coming winter season, frequent attention was again given to golf. Although the clubhouse, professional's shop, and locker house were not open, the greens were excellent, leading to a good and early start for the sport.

On October 9, the major feature article in the *Miami Daily Metropolis* discussed events in Miami Beach. A section on the Flamingo Hotel noted that the Flamingo's nine-hole golf course had been designed and constructed by Lee Nelson and that it would have its own professional golf instructors. Fisher announced that he expected the new 18-hole Bay Shore course to be completed by January 1, 1921.

Neither the clubhouse nor the golf course for the Miami Beach Bay Shore golf club would be completed by January 1, but the Miami Beach Golf and Country Club was busy. On November 7, 1920, T.W. Palmer and Henry Ralston were playing when they noticed two of the Nelson brothers passing by and asked the brothers to play them. The Nelsons kidded the Miami pair that they were not much into hobnobbing with pale-faced brokers and profiteers, but they would take on the pair for 18 holes. The Nelsons eclipsed Palmer-Ralston, with E.R. Nelson making a 72, three under par, and brother F.E. Nelson being close to par.

An announcement on December 30 claimed that there was three times as much golf playing as there had been by that date in the previous year and that about 75 percent of the players were tourists. The golf club was being redecorated for the opening of the tearoom on January 1 with the tearoom being moved from the porch to indoors. The new lockers, replacing those that burned in April, were finally completed.

Over near the Flamingo Hotel, the nine-hole course was almost finished. Marquees had been raised and plans were being made for someone to play the course to figure out a par for the course. The gondolas that would carry guests to the golf fields and other places had been ordered, and plans called for "Big Bahamian negroes who can scull" to operate the gondolas. The social and fashion interests continued, with frequent fashion statements about women on the golf links. As usual, some individual golfers got their names in the newspaper.

Of course, locals were still playing. On December 12, for example, one of the locals on the golf course was Louis F. Snedigar. A couple of weeks later, on December 30, Mrs. Louis Snedigar was expected to return to Miami Beach from the hospital in Miami with their new little son Louis Jr. Two years later, Louis F. "Red" Snedigar would be elected Miami Beach's fourth mayor. Serving from December 1922 to December 1926, December 1928 to December 1930, and December 1934 to June 1937, he still remains Miami Beach's longest-serving mayor. And in a colorful city, he was one of the most colorful mayors. Almost 80 years later, on November 20, 2000, another son, James M. Snedigar, would be the first speaker of the newly formed Miami Beach Historical Association.

The six Nelson brothers, including Lee, who was in charge of the Miami Beach Golf and Country Club, were recognized as the largest family of golf professionals in the United States. Golf remained popular, even on rainy days. The week of December 19 started off with a bang when Erwin Nelson, one of the brothers, took 18 holes in 70, two below par. The *Miami Metropolis* wrote that "Who's Who" on the golf course is always interesting and mentioned United States Senator A.B.

Golfers and caddies are shown here at the Miami Beach Golf and Country Club. Note the extent to which golfers dressed up while playing.

Cummins of Iowa, who was staying at the Lincoln Hotel across the road from the golf course.

On December 22, for the first time in the current season at the Miami Beach Golf and Country Club, the full 18 holes were opened, 10 holes on the south side of the Collins Canal, and 8 holes on the north side, which had not yet been used because a barge had damaged the bridge at the west end of the course. Erwin Nelson reported that 3 holes had been changed on the north side, that the 12th, 13th, and 17th holes had been lengthened, and that 3 new greens had been made. There was more rolling ground and less dog-legged holes.

Most of the golfers were men. There were a few female golfers, but women were more likely to participate as spectators, with a heavy emphasis on socialization and fashion. Horse riding on bridal paths was popular for women, as was swimming and, to some degree, tennis playing. On December 29, when many of the men from the local area had gone on a special boat trip to Havana with Carl Fisher, foursomes and threesomes were mostly feminine affairs. However, while local male club members were mostly absent, a number of visiting men still played. On the next to last day of 1920, more out-of-town visitors registered at the golf club than during any previous day of the season and 30 golfers were listed in the newspaper. They represented nine states and the District of Columbia. Two winter residents of Miami Beach were also listed.

Because there were a number of local residents who also liked the Miami Beach course, on December 21, 1920, Thomas J. Pancoast (who two months earlier had finished a term as mayor of Miami Beach) of the Miami Beach Improvement

The speedboat Marycel *passes the grandstand at the Mid-winter Regatta on Miami Beach. On March 5, Hoosier V set a world's record for the 10-mile express cruiser race with an average speed of 31.3 miles per hour.*

Company, which managed the Collins Bridge, lowered the toll on the bridge to encourage more golfers to use it instead of the free County Causeway that had opened earlier in the year. He stated that the distance from Miami to the Miami Beach Baths and the golf course was 5 miles less by way of the Collins Bridge than by the causeway. Pancoast estimated the cost of gasoline and oil at about 75¢ for the 5 miles and lowered the toll from 20¢ each way to 15¢ one way or 25¢ for a round trip. Congestion on the causeway at certain times was another reason golfers sometimes preferred to use the Collins Bridge.

The 1921 Florida State Golf Association tournament was scheduled at the old Miami Beach Golf and Country Club course in April 1921, with 150 players to start in the championship competition. R.B. Burdine of Miami was president of the association. The golf future at Miami Beach looked great as 1920 ended.

The motorboat was invented in 1887 by Gottlieb Daimler, who had also "invented" the motorcycle in 1885 by attaching an internal combustion engine to a bicycle, though it was about 1900 before any further interest was shown in motorboats. In 1903, in New York, 20 yacht clubs organized the American Power Boat Association (APBA). The association's first major sport was held in June 1904 and boat racing (regattas) became popular. Powerboats, like sail yachts, were mostly custom-made until mass production began in the 1920s. Carl Fisher's love of speed (as shown by his background in automobile racing), the availability of water around Miami Beach, and the fact that powerboat racing was an expensive sport for the well-off combined to make regattas a major love for Fisher and a major sport to fit into Fisher's vision for Miami Beach. It did not receive as much publicity as polo and golf received, but it was an important part of Miami Beach's sports life.

The Sixth Annual Mid-winter Regatta was one of the most popular special events in Miami Beach in 1920. As the new year began, the local papers announced that the Annual Mid-winter Regatta would be held on March 5 and 6. The races were scheduled later than usual "so as to better arrange the entire sporting calendar of events at the beach." Rules required that before a speedboat could enter the regatta, it had to finish either a long-distance race from the Biscayne Bay Yacht Club in Miami to Gun Key (Bimini) and return to Government Cut on February 14 (106 miles), a similar race to Palm Beach and return on February 21 (138 miles), or a similar race to Key West and return on February 28 (157 miles).

On February 14, the County Causeway, which was not yet opened to traffic, was opened on both the Miami and Miami Beach sides for foot passengers only to view the race. Because the return trip ended at the bay line of Government Cut, hundreds of people gathered at Hardie's Casino and Smith's Casino, swimming in the surf or pools while waiting for the end. Some people took a hasty lunch at Smith's, probably enjoying the cooking of Joe Weiss while waiting. The greatest concern was raised when Gar Wood, one of the most popular boat racers, disappeared. A search party didn't find him. Wood showed up later, explaining that he had experienced various troubles on his return trip from Bimini and that he and the other boats simply had not crossed paths.

Gar Wood was a very big name in boat racing and his participation in Miami Beach regattas indicated how important the Miami Beach races were. He was considered the pioneer of powerboat racing off the shores of Miami Beach and was known as the "speedboat king." He won eight consecutive international Harmsworth Trophies, four United States Gold Cups, and held five world championship records for boat racing. Wood is credited with designing what later became the PT boat of World War II. With his new industrial wealth and his love for the relatively new sport of boating racing, Wood was exactly the type of person Fisher wanted to attract to Miami Beach. In 1951, 12 years after Fisher's death, Wood would own most of Fisher Island and would successfully have his part of Fisher Island moved from Miami Beach to Miami jurisdiction.

The other two preliminaries were held as scheduled, although tragedy was narrowly averted during the race to Key West when two of the boats hit a submerged wreck near Caesar's Creek. Both the *Gar Jr.*, owned by Gar Wood, and the *Hoosier V*, owned by Miami Beach winter resident H.R. Duckwall, were damaged, as was the boat (with a broken propeller) owned by another winter resident, Arthur C. Newby. Carl Fisher's *Shadow V* won.

As the regatta approached, the *Miami Herald* reported that Purdy's boatyard at Miami Beach was a busy place. Nearly all of the fast power boats that would appear in the Miami Mid-winter Regatta were at anchor receiving their final touches. The street next to Purdy's boatyard would become Purdy Road and is now Sunset Harbour Drive.

Because the new County Causeway had opened to traffic on February 17, sightseers were expected to arrive over both the causeway and Collins Bridge, making traffic regulations more difficult than before. Motorists were encouraged to use the Collins Bridge because the new causeway was not totally completed and because the right-of-way enjoyed by watercraft would cause traffic delays. Nonetheless, as feared by officials, nine out of ten vehicles took the causeway and suffered considerable delays.

Officials said it was difficult to estimate attendance on Friday, March 5, the first day, though it was the largest attendance at the annual regatta in its six years of existence. Three world's records were shattered and spectators were also entertained by flying stunts of various planes from small baby planes to large "flying boats."

The *Miami Herald* was explosive in its praise of Miami Beach's Sixth Annual Regatta, noting that there was no doubt that the regatta was one of the most brilliant spectacles ever displayed in the world! The two newspapers were great boosters of Miami Beach. Eight more world's records were broken the second day and then Miami Beach really celebrated. A black-and-white ball was held at the Miami Beach Casino on Saturday night, with extra buses running before and after the dancing in order to give all an opportunity to take part. On the following Tuesday night, March 9, what promised to be the crowning entertainment of the Miami Beach casino season was the yachtsman's ball where awards were to be presented to those who won races at the regatta. Actually, most of the winners did not attend the ball, although one writer suggested that it was because they were too modest to appear in person.

As late 1920 approached, Fisher began to think of the 1921 regatta. Fisher actively took part in several sports, but boat racing was his favorite, according to his wife, Jane. His nickname was Skipper, which was given him as a boy because of his passion for boats. Despite his love of boating and regattas, Fisher also was a brilliant realist. During the March 1920 regatta, considerable damage had been done to the growing trees and Fisher predicted that it would be only a year or two before residents would begin complaining of a nuisance. The regatta would last only a few more years.

Polo, golf, and boating regattas comprised the major sports for tourists in Miami Beach in 1920, but tennis, swimming, fishing, seaplane flying, and horseback riding also had followers. The public tennis court was run down, but Fisher built private indoor tennis courts on Lincoln Road and hired Charles E. Haggett, referred to as the finest tennis player in the world, as manager. Fisher was also building clay and sand tennis courts at the Flamingo Hotel. Of course, swimming was a sport in Miami Beach, situated between a bay and an ocean. The major event was the New Year's Cross-Bay Swim each January 1, across Biscayne Bay from Miami to Miami Beach. As seen elsewhere in this book, there also were frequent swimming contests at the casinos and the bath club and, of course, swimming was a major activity at the ocean.

Swimmers prepare for the Cross-Bay swim on January 1, 1920. Miss Francis Bilsbarrow, lifeguard at the Miami Beach Baths, was the winner, finishing in 1 hour, 36.5 minutes.

Fishing was very popular in 1920 Miami Beach, with local people generally preferring fishing in the bay and tourists frequently going on chartered deep-sea fishing trips. The Miami Angler's Club made frequent trips to Bimini, which were especially popular after Prohibition. Locals fished for both pleasure and food, while tourists put more emphasis on pleasure only. City councilman Charles Meloy was one of the most popular local charter boat captains. Also, as seen in this book, seaplane flying was popular, with frequent local trips being made for fun and sightseeing from the Breakers Hotel and from casinos. However, opposition arose to the noise, and the continuation of flights was in doubt. Jane Fisher was interested in horseback riding, so Carl made plans to build a 9-mile-long bridle path, 12 feet wide. Four miles had been completed by the end of 1920 and, occasionally, the newspapers listed women who were riding. Trap shooting was also popular, with at least two shooting traps on Ocean Drive. Clay targets were used.

On October 9, the *Miami Daily Metropolis* published an article entitled "Miami Beach is the Sportsman's Paradise in Summer and Winter." With support from tourists, local people, and Carl Fisher, this was certainly a true statement. Miami was already the site of a professional baseball team's summer training camp, but baseball and other traditional team sports were not big in Miami Beach. With Fisher's vision and backing for Miami Beach as a resort and home for the wealthy, and with a bay on one side and an ocean on the other side, Miami Beach had a special orientation in sports, especially the "prestigious" ones.

Trapshooting was popular in Miami Beach in 1920. This photo was probably taken on Ocean Drive around Second or Third Streets.

8. DAILY LIFE IN MIAMI BEACH IN 1920

As we have seen, sports played a major part in the lives of tourists and residents in 1920 Miami Beach. Polo, golf, tennis, boating, fishing, swimming, aeroplane flying, horseback riding, trapshooting, and other sports provided choices for everybody. Some of the sports also doubled as social life, and much of social life also evolved around the Miami Beach Casino, the Miami Beach Club, Hardie's Casino, Smith's Casino, Brown's Hotel, and other settings. Special occasions included the Palm Fete in late December, the swim across the bay on New Year's Day, the annual boating regatta during the first part of the year, some of the United States holidays (which varied in the extent of celebration from year to year because of the ban on Sunday fun), swimming matches at the casinos, and competitions in many sports. Miami Beach was a resort, and it provided entertainment for those in the city. Local residents, many of whom worked hard during the winter tourist season, frequently traveled themselves during much of the long summer, which could go from around May until mid-September and, in 1920, until early October. Many spent part of the summer in cooler settings, such as the mountains of North Carolina, but recognizing that few Miami Beach residents originally came from the Miami area, many also visited relatives and friends in their former homes.

As a new town with so much emphasis on sports and fun for tourists and winter residents, cultural life was just beginning in 1920. Fisher announced early that year that he planned to build the Altonia theater, designed by the noted local architect August Geiger, on the northwest corner of Lincoln Road and James Street, with orchestra, balcony, and box seats totaling about 1,000. By mid-December, Fisher acknowledged that he had delayed construction on the theater because he had too many other projects in progress and that, for 1920, Miami Beach would not have a movie theater. Although the Selznick Pictures Corporation was shooting pictures in Miami Beach in 1920, and although Earle Emlay had shot Miami Beach movies and had created a great sensation in New York, there was not a theatre in Miami Beach in which to see them. Miami Beach people had to go to Miami to see the movies made in their own town because the town was growing too fast to have time to build a movie theatre and, as noted, they also had to go to Miami to enjoy live theater.

Educational life and religious life were also still developing in Miami Beach in 1920. As the year began, public school children in Miami Beach still had to go to schools in Miami. In March 1920, construction on a school in Miami Beach, with Spanish Mission architecture, was started without sufficient funds to complete it. In May, the entire county voted 113 to 12 to fund school construction in the county because growth was so great that children were being educated in tents, but this was not enough to complete Miami Beach's school. Carl Fisher advanced money to finish the construction, and the school was named the Ida M. Fisher School in honor of Carl's mother. Miami Beach also had successfully pushed for a kindergarten.

The school finally opened on October 11, late because of construction problems and problems finding teachers. There was a national shortage of teachers—they were poorly paid—and at Homestead, in southern Dade County, teachers almost went on strike over teaching conditions. The Miami Beach school actually was less crowded than other county schools.

Teachers were instructed to begin the day with appropriate religious services and to use little powder on their noses and no paint on their cheeks. By early November, a Miami Beach Parent Teacher Association (PTA) had been organized and became active in the community's educational life. A group of students performed in the Palm Fete in December, marching through downtown Miami and performing a Dutch dance. Illustrating the city's tremendous growth, only 9 of the 33 children listed as participating in the Palm Fete had lived in Miami Beach in January 1920 when the census was taken. The school was expected to attract even more people to Miami Beach. For example, Mr. and Mrs. Moses Goldenberg of Canada lived in Miami Beach during the 1919–1920 winter season and said that they might return with their children for the next winter season because of the availability of an elementary school.

Private schools were also important to Miami Beach in 1920, not only because of the lack of a public school, but because many winter residents needed to make

Montemare School was the second private school in Miami Beach, opening in early 1921 after Thomas J. Pancoast spruced up his home and built a classroom in 1920. (Miami Herald.)

Ida M. Fisher Elementary School, which opened in October 1920, is still serving as a school. Here, the building appears about completed, but the grounds are not, suggesting that this photograph was taken about September or October of 1920. H. George Fink designed the school in Spanish Mission style.

special arrangements. The Eunice Martin School had been built especially for the accommodation of tourists at the instigation of Carl Fisher. It had opened in the winter of 1916 with four students and had moved to the northwest corner of Lincoln Road and Jefferson Avenue. It finished its fourth year on May 7, 1920 with 50 students and opened for its fifth year on December 6, 1920.

Plans for another private school, Montemare, were announced in March 1920. It was to be a "high class" college preparatory boarding school for girls aged 12 to 20, eighth grade through high school, to run from January 1 until Easter at the Thomas J. Pancoast residence and adjoining cottages on Collins Avenue. Fall and spring classes were to be held in Lake Placid, New York. Similar to the Lake Placid and Adirondack-Florida school for boys, which held its winter term a few miles away in Coconut Grove, emphasis was to be put on tennis, boating, swimming, and outdoor life in general. Sailing, canoeing, and weekend cruises were also included. The school would open on January 10, 1921 when some pupils with chaperones arrived on the morning trains. It was noted that the school affairs would be "quite important" because the members of the school were from exclusive New York families.

The city did not yet have a library, although Mayor Pancoast at least implied the need for one at a city council meeting on August 13 when, during discussion of a

The site of much gambling and alcohol drinking, the famous Jungle Inn was raided on February 3, 1921 by a newly elected sheriff.

controversial tract of land being given to the city by the Collins and Pancoast real estate interests, he noted that the land was to be used for park purposes only "with the possible exception of its later becoming a site for Public Library or Convention Hall."

Religious life was also just developing in Miami Beach in 1920. There had been small Protestant Sunday school meetings in Smith's Casino in 1917, but those meetings apparently ended. In February 1919, nine people met at City Hall to begin plans for organizing another Sunday school and this would lead to the organization of the Miami Beach Congregational Church on Lincoln Road. The first service was held at the Eunice Martin School on Lincoln Road on January 4, 1920, with 38 people attending. The Congregationalists had already started building a church on Lincoln Road and, on March 14, the group began holding Sunday religious services in the uncompleted building. The building was designed in the Spanish style by noted local architecture Walter C. DeGarmo. The church was delayed from opening in December because the pastor was sick but was dedicated in early 1921. The church congregation hoped to be a union church for the community and, by late 1921, was viewed as a nondenominational church.

There was not a Catholic church in Miami Beach in 1920, and the Church of the Holy Name in Miami was too small to accommodate the increasing number of local and winter residents and tourists. The first Catholic mass celebrated in Miami Beach was by Father William Barry, the tourist priest, in a converted polo stable Fisher had given to Barry. There would not be a Catholic church until 1926 with the founding of St. Patrick's Catholic Church.

There were only a few Jewish residents in Miami Beach in 1920 and a significant number of Jewish tourists and winter residents, but there was not a Jewish house of worship. There was an active religious and social life in Miami with frequent services, special ceremonies, a women's group, and guest speakers. Miami Beach's first synagogue, Beth Jacob, was not built until 1927.

There was a brief reference to Latter Day Saints (Mormons) holding services in the A.L. Johnson home in Miami Beach in 1920. By August 8, attendance was 40 and the group began expressing interest in buying land to build their own chapel. Protestant churches were racially segregated in 1920 and the approximately 40 blacks in Miami Beach, mostly Protestants from the southern United States or the Bahamas, also had to go to Miami for services. Occasionally, other religious services were held and attracted attention. In July, the Pentecostal Church of Miami baptized six converts at Fourth Street and the ocean, with 50 church members and many spectators present.

Two hot issues in the United States in 1920 were Prohibition, which took effect on January 16, 1920, and women's suffrage, which took effect on August 18, 1920. Both were relevant to Miami Beach to varying degrees, but Prohibition by far received the most attention. Prohibition was a major issue in Dade County and both local newspapers took sides. As noted, the *Miami Metropolis* generally supported it and the *Miami Herald* was generally opposed. When the county Republican party held a rally at Smith's Casino on October 27, the Republicans accused the Democratic county officials of not enforcing the liquor laws. Frequent references were made in the newspapers about alcohol-related activities in Miami and several incidents referred to were in Miami Beach. On March 11, the *Miami Metropolis* announced that, some distance west of the old life-saving station at Miami Beach, there was a lonesome log house where alcohol was served and gambling took place. The *Metropolis* sent a reporter called "Madge" to find the club called the Jungle Inn. She wrote an exposé article and the club was raided in early 1921. Actually, the club was outside of Miami Beach's city limits, but it brought publicity to Miami Beach.

In late August, the chairman of the South End Club accused some Miami Beach councilmen of "possessing knowledge in regard to bootlegging which they shut their eyes to," and the new city council, which took office in October, appeared to be tougher on bootlegging. On November 18, two men, who had been arrested for unloading liquor at the mouth of Indian Creek, broke out of the Miami Beach jail. As a result of the jailbreak, Andre de Monceaux, a police officer and a popular man about town, resigned. Soon, he was apppointed a mounted officer for the Flamingo Polo Club grounds, one of Carl Fisher's undertakings. The city judge had a case involving the "Coney Island Restaurant man" who ran a restaurant on South Beach and was accused of selling alcohol. As the year ended, this case was still unresolved.

Fisher was strongly opposed to Prohibition. He was not a heavy drinker before Prohibition, but he was a self-made man who strongly believed in individual rights and strongly resented the government's intrusion into people's personal lives. Several letters in his files show his involvement in illegal alcohol activities in 1920. On April 5, Fisher got a letter from his good friend James A. Allison, who was building the aquarium in Miami Beach, telling Fisher that when he was in Washington he had received a tip that Secret Service men were in Miami looking around. He continued to say, "So it might be a pretty good idea to have anything that your friends may own placed in a safe place. I think that Peterson is putting everything I am interested in in the new storage place, where I think it will be all right." On April 28, Fisher wrote Allison that Revenue Officers had discovered Allison's secret hiding place at the aquarium, that the Revenue Officer had told him that it was the second largest haul they had ever made, but that the *Miami Herald* had treated the matter very decently. Several years later, Fisher wrote a Republican congressman from New York that he was going to become a Democrat if the Republicans did not stop their support of Prohibition.

By 1922, Kenneth L. Roberts would write that there was no room at Miami Beach for killing time because "There is something doing every minute. There is golf and tennis and polo and bathing and dancing and seeing the bootlegger, or rushing over to town [Miami] to see a movie or an orange grove or another bootlegger or something."[1]

An anti-cigarette movement had existed in the United States for decades and, by the first decade of the 1900s, cigarette smoking was banned in many areas of the country. Before World War I, smoking had been a habit mostly of upper-class "respectable" men. As more women and working-class men started smoking, opposition increased. Beginning largely in 1920, women began to smoke in public for the first time, considering it a mark of equality with men. In the Miami Beach area, however, little newspaper attention was given to cigarettes except to smoking by public school students and to the increase in cigarette smoking by both male and female students. A county school official noted that the habit was growing at a rapid rate for both boys and girls. He wanted a copy of the law and penalty against cigarettes printed on strong cardboard, distributed to every dealer, and posted in a conspicuous place so that the dealer could not plead ignorance.

Women received the right to vote in all parts of the United States on August 18, 1920, and a number of women began registering to vote in the county and in Miami Beach. In Dade County, there was much discussion about female voters, with racism being a big part of the picture. The Women Voters' League, at a mass meeting on October 15, had a speaker who made it clear that her theme was white supremacy. On November 1, the day before the national election, the Women's Democratic Auxiliary took out a large boxed advertisement "To the Woman Voter" in the *Miami Metropolis*, saying that they were "standing squarely, shoulder to shoulder, with the Democratic men of Dade County in their fight to maintain white supremacy." Both the Democratic and Republicans parties tried to get the women's vote. On the day of the presidential election, "Vote Early and Vote Straight!" in the *Miami Herald* told men and women that, other than the personal equation, there was only one issue—"shall the white race continue in power?"

Compared to the county, the political situation in Miami Beach was calm. The South End Club, the political civic club in Miami Beach, invited women to a mass meeting on October 4, sponsored a Ladies Night at Smith's Casino, attended a reciprocal function at Smith's Casino sponsored for men by women, and soon voted itself out of existence partly because it recognized that a male-only club was no longer feasible. On October 25, eight days before the presidential election, Miami Beach had a city election and women voted for the first time. By that time, there were 124 males and 51 females registered, with the females comprising 29 percent. Every woman who had registered voted except one. That one was Mrs. Lura (Herman) Scheibli, who was out of town. She was the person who had written a letter on August 9 to wearers of skimpy bathing suits saying that they were guilty only of poor judgment. The *Miami Daily Metropolis* noted on October 26 that "Most of the women made it an afternoon affair, coming down to the polls between 3 and 5 o'clock. All that was lacking to make a fashionable affair was tea and cakes." The city leaders wanted to make a good impression on women, so booths had been constructed for women voters, with curtains, and officials made sure that the voting area was clean and in good order. Women were described as very earnest and independent and not asking for any instructions from male inspectors or election officials.

As discussed earlier, the one gender issue that was controversial in Miami Beach in 1920 concerned female bathing suits, but the women in Miami Beach had diverse opinions on this issue. The lines were drawn more between traditionalists

Located on Biscayne Bay next to the County Causeway, the aquarium was famous for its exhibition of fish, scientific research on fish, and Jim Allison's secret hiding place for liquor, which was raided in April 1921.

and modernists than between males and females as the 1920s began. The meaning of morality was becoming more subjective in the decade that followed the ending of the war in 1919. A new generation was in the making and was described colorfully as

> a breed of youngsters who claimed to be hardboiled, heavy-drinking and daring—and sometimes were. The girls in particular seemed to have changed . . . The advent of Prohibition made clandestine drinking an appealing game; women took up the sport alongside men. They also took up smoking; sales of cigarettes doubled during the decade. Morals were undergoing a revolution.[2]

This was the beginning of changes in values that would lead to the Roaring Twenties. There is disagreement over the meaning of decadent and proper, but certainly Miami Beach was coming of age in an exciting time.

In the United States in 1920, the average income was $2,160, a new house averaged $6,296, a new car cost about $1,300 to $2,000, a loaf of bread cost 11¢, a quart of milk was 17¢, a gallon of gas was 30¢, and a postage stamp was 2¢. Miami Beach residents still generally had to go to Miami for clothes, furniture, food, and other essentials. There, they could buy two cans of Campbell soups for 25¢, a package of Corn Flakes for 18¢, a pound of Maxwell House coffee for 43¢, a pound of lard for 17¢, 6 pounds of grits for 25¢, a pound of onions for 5¢, a best grade pound of ham for 35¢, a sugar-cured pound of picnic ham for 30¢, and a fat

This was the rear view of Carl and Jane Fisher's home on Lincoln Road and the Atlantic Ocean. The front side, with a curved porch, faced the ocean.

2-pound Salt Mackerel for 45¢. Miami Beach was slowly developing a business district and a number of homes for permanent residents in 1920, but tourism remained the main attraction.

In 1920, as in all years, Miami Beach greatly publicized its two natural attractions, the ocean and the relatively warm winter weather. The coldest day recorded at Miami in 1920 was March 2, at 34 degrees Fahrenheit. The freezing point was not reached in 1920, although below-freezing temperatures were recorded in rural areas further inland. The highest temperature, 89 degrees, was recorded on September 14. Overall, the year had less rain than usual, 47.6 inches, and was described as dryer and a little cooler than usual. In the middle of June, for example, the *Miami Herald* claimed that the summer climate in Miami was the envy of the eastern half of the United States and listed other cities that had hotter summers. The wind could be too much around March and April, especially in the sandy parts of new earth that did not yet have trees, grass, or weeds, and there was frequent complaining among the local residents about mosquitoes. On August 13, the city council discussed, but did not act on, a suggestion to hire at least one person full-time to eliminate mosquitoes. The warm weather led to weeds galore, especially with so many absentee lot owners and, on July 21, the city council hired a man at $2.25 per lot to clear weeds and rubbish. These were local issues, though, and seldom made the tourist-oriented press.

Throughout the year, numerous newspaper articles referred to the beautiful weather, with an occasional mention of a few rainy days or more wind than some people preferred. Fisher planned to construct a large thermometer, regulated and tested by the government, so that daily readings could be taken, recorded, and, of course, publicized nationally. Weather was one of Miami Beach's greatest attractions and Fisher wanted to make sure that everybody knew it. Marjory Stoneman Douglas, the local area's suffragist, environmentalist, and outspoken columnist for the *Miami Herald*, did not like Fisher because of his developments, but she agreed with Fisher on two major issues, Prohibition and the weather. In 1920, she wrote in the *Miami Herald* that "It seems exceedingly difficult for northerners to get any idea of Florida's mean temperature until they get here, when they learn, to their joy, that no temperature in Florida is ever mean."[3] Perhaps Fisher and Douglas overstated the point a little, but the weather certainly was a great benefit for Miami Beach.

Epilogue

Miami Beach has had a roller-coaster life since 1920 when its population was about 641. In the years following 1920, the city continued growing rapidly. Only five years later, in 1925, the population had almost quadrupled to 2,342. The hurricane of 1926 destroyed much of the Miami area, but Miami Beach's population still increased to 6,494 by 1930, ten times what it had been only ten years earlier. The Great Depression, which began in 1929, caused serious problems in Miami Beach, but the problems were not as serious as in most of the United States, and the population increased again to 13,330 by 1935. By 1940, the number of people had doubled to 28,012, over four times what it had been in 1930. One of the nation's largest army training camps was located in Miami Beach during World War II and, after the war, many veterans returned to live in the area.

By 1950, partly because of Miami Beach's importance in training for the war, the local population had increased 65 percent in the 1940s decade to 46,282. The rate of growth slowed in the 1950s, but by 1960, the population still had increased to 63,145, one-third more than it had been in 1950. In the 1960s, the rate of growth continued at about one-third to 87,072 in 1970. The 1960s also saw a major age change in the city, with the percentage of elderly (age 65 and over) increasing from 28.2 percent of the population in 1960 to 48.7 percent in 1970. By the 1970s, however, as Miami Beach became a major retirement center for the elderly, the growth rate slowed. By 1980, largely because of a high death rate from the high percentage of older citizens, the population increased only to 96,298, and 51.8 percent of the residents were over age 65.

In the last few years of the 1980s and continuing throughout the 1990s, there was a major gentrification movement in Miami Beach, largely based on the popularity of Art Deco Architecture and the changes it brought in national and international tourism, as well as modeling, movie and television production, and related areas. There continued to be a high death rate among the elderly, many elderly left the community as prices increased, small apartments frequently were combined into larger, much more expensive apartments, and vast numbers of young people started moving in. By 1990, the population had decreased to 92,296 and the elderly comprised only 30 percent. With the continuation of gentrification, there was another major decrease in the 1990s in both population

BEAUTIFUL BELLE ISLE

I HAVE SEVERAL EXCLUSIVE RESIDENTIAL LOTS LOCATED ON BELLE ISLE FOR SALE

All lots have full riparian rights and full ownership privileges of the beautiful private park in the center of the isle. Prices range from $165 to $200 per front foot and are safely $50 per front foot less than any other bay front property as ideally located on Miami Beach. These are last year's prices and will be advanced 10 per cent on January 10th.

One-fifth Cash and Very Satisfactory Terms May Be Arranged on the Balance

JAMES F. MATHEWS

Fidelity Bank Bldg., or Residence on Belle Isle   Phone 198

ALL MEMBERS OF REALTY BOARD ARE INVITED TO CO-OPERATE

*Belle Isle was one of the hot areas for palatial homes. James F. Mathews reported that his father was born in Cuba and spoke Spanish as his native language. (*Miami Herald.*)*

size and percentage of elderly. By 2000, the number of residents was 87,933 and the percentage of residents age 65 and over was only 19 percent. Miami Beach had undergone a major demographic change regarding the age composition of the city and the gentrification continues. South Beach, the southern end of the city, achieved world-wide fame as SoBe, a hot spot for entertainment, the media, and fashion.

Miami Beach also has undergone two ethnic successions since 1920. When the census was taken in early 1920, the city was very diverse in geographic origins, but very homogeneous in ethnicity. Of 641 residents, only 2 were known to be Jewish (and possibly a few others), no Hispanics were in residence (unless the count includes James F. Mathews, a broker and realtor who lived on Belle Isle and told the census taker that his father had been born in Cuba and spoke Spanish as his native language), 39 blacks (about two-thirds from the Bahamas and most of the others from the southern United States), and 4 Japanese (at least 2 had been recruited by Fisher to work in landscaping). Canada was the birthplace of 7 people and 45 had been born in Europe, most in western Europe. The combined Jewish, Hispanic, black, and Japanese residents accounted for about 7 percent of the population and "Anglo" Christians, mostly Protestants, made up about 93 percent.

The city remained a largely white Protestant community until the 1940s. In 1940, Jewish residents accounted for only about 16 percent of the city's population, but by 1950, the percentage was 52 percent. By 1960, Jewish residents accounted for 73 percent, and by 1970, 80 percent. The Jewish percentage overlapped heavily with the elderly percentage. By 1980, the Jewish percentage was down to 66 percent, and by 1990, it was down even more to 40 percent, and probably has decreased since then to about one-third of the population. Part of the reason for the decrease in the percentage of Jewish residents was the rapid growth of the Hispanic and, especially, the Cuban-American population. In 1960, Hispanics accounted for only 1 percent of Miami Beach's population, but following the mass migration from Cuba to the Miami area that began as a result

Miami Beach's first post office was opened on December 4, 1920, on Fifth Street. It was demolished on November 5, 1997, shortly after the city's Historic Preservation Board recommended designation as a historic building and site but before the City Commission could act on the recommendation. This photo was taken May 19, 1921.

of Fidel Castro's dictatorship, Hispanics comprised 10 percent of Miami Beach's population in 1970. By 1980, Hispanics accounted for 22 percent of the city's population; by 1990, 47 percent and, by 2000, 53 percent. Now, about half of the Hispanics are non-Cuban.

As Miami Beach underwent major demographic changes since 1920, it also altered its status as a resort city. After its great growth in the year 1920, Miami Beach continued booming. Although the hurricane of 1926 set the city back and the Depression hurt, by the mid-1930s, building permits were soaring. During World War II, from February 1942 through December 1945, most hotels in Miami Beach were taken over by the United States Army and Miami Beach became a major military training area. Over 500,000 Army Air Corps soldiers trained on Miami Beach during World War II. After undergoing the post-war building boom, by the late 1940s and the 1950s, Miami Beach had again become "America's Playground." Affordable airplane flights and air conditioning were also major factors in the city's resurgence. This time, however, the city also became a major center for gamblers and organized crime. These largely ended by the early 1950s, after the Kefauver Committee's investigation in 1950, but Miami Beach remained popular as a vacation spot.

The boom continued into the 1960s, but by the 1970s, Miami Beach had peaked and was beginning to lose its luster. Miami Beach's image as an elderly resort (and, some say, as a "Jewish city") were hurting the city's image as a winter vacation resort city. Nevertheless, Miami Beach's unique Art Deco architecture had been "discovered" in December 1976 by Barbara Capitman and the architecture soon became the basis of the rebirth of the city's attraction as a tourist city. Capitman died March 29, 1990, 11 days short of her 70th birthday, "an elderly Jewish woman." The Miami Design Preservation League played the leading role in fighting for historic preservation.

As this book is written, Miami Beach is, as a result of gentrification, once again a major resort city with a year-round reputation among tourists from Europe, Latin America, and other parts of the world. Major modeling and movie production agencies have brought the city tremendous national and international publicity. Miami Beach has also begun to develop a business economy with Internet, entertainment, and new-media emphases, as well as more traditional businesses.

The Flamingo Golf Course has been a city park since 1930. Part of the original golf course of the Miami Beach Golf and Country Club remains, but much of the golf course now is occupied by buildings. For years, Morton Towers was situated on the location of the demolished Flamingo Hotel, but now the site has been reborn as the Grand Flamingo Apartments on the Bay, with 1,670 apartments and town homes. The building that housed the original Joe's Restaurant has been replaced by a much larger building, but Joe's Stone Crab Restaurant remains as one of Miami Beach's classics. The city's first post office, built on Fifth Street in 1920, was demolished on November 5, 1997, a month short of its 77th birthday. The clubhouse for the Miami Beach Golf Club, Brown's Hotel, Ida M. Fisher Elementary School, the Congregational Church on Lincoln Mall, Avery Smith's home on the northwest corner of Collins Avenue and Ninth Street, and a small number of other structures built before or during 1920 still stand. However, most of Miami Beach's early buildings have long been demolished to make room for larger structures. Miami Beach now has numerous luxury high rises and there is a constant battle between those who want more and those who want to keep a smaller scale.

As this book goes to press in 2002, the future for Miami Beach looks great. The fame of SoBe continues and the city is also building a solid residential and business base. Miami Beach has become a model for ethnic relations in Miami–Dade County, successfully avoiding ethnic divisiveness and rigid ethnic voting that pervades much of the county. The youthful Mayor David Dermer, elected in 2001 and the son of Jay Dermer, who served as mayor from 1967 to 1971 (the only father-son mayors since J.N. Lummus, the first mayor from 1915 to 1918, and his son J.N. Jr., from 1926 to 1928), heads a seven-person mayor-commission form of government. It has four Jewish members and four Hispanic members, including one commissioner who is both Hispanic and Jewish. The city has a long history of hiring people of diverse ethnic identities to run the city departments on a daily basis.

In 1992, Miami Beach was one of the first areas in the nation to adopt a Human Rights Ordinance regarding sexual orientation, and the mayor and commissioners strongly support diversity and tolerance. Governmental corruption has been common in the county, but Miami Beach is the comparative model of good government with strong laws for open government. The city has taken a progressive stand on historical preservation, first with Art Deco and now with Miami Modernism, MiMo. In his State of the City Address on March 26, 2002, the city's 87th birthday, Mayor David Dermer noted that "Miami Beach is a city that has built a legacy of upholding tradition and heritage." In recent years, strong efforts have been made to preserve open space and limit the height of future buildings. The building of recreational facilities to improve the quality of life has a high priority. The city is one of the most active special events communities in the nation and strongly encourages cultural arts. From grits and bacon, to lox and bagels, to arroz con pollo, Miami Beach remains a truly amazing city.

Avery C. and Edna Smith, Edna's mother Minnie Aling, and four-year-old Avery C. Jr. lived at this home on the northwest corner of Collins Avenue and Ninth Street. The building remains one of Miami Beach's best examples of early architecture.

ENDNOTES

1. EARLY HISTORY

1. Miami Beach Chamber of Commerce, "Brief History of Miami Beach," 1958.

2. THE PROBLEM OF ROADS

1. Wynne, Nick. *Tin Can Tourists in Florida 1900–1970*, p. 7.
2. "Auto Tourists Migrate South," *Miami Herald*, December 25, 1920, p. 12.
3. "Thrilling is Rescue of Girl Who Fell From Causeway," *Miami Daily Metropolis*, June 16, 1920, p. 1.
4. "Trial Trip of Beach Street Car Indicates Need of New Rulings," *Miami Metropolis*, December 15, 1920, p. 4.

3. ON THE RAILS, ON THE WATER, IN THE AIR

1. Harger, Line. "Business Men's Excursion to Havana Shows Possibilities of Trade With West Indies," *Miami Metropolis*, January 1, 1921, p. 3.
2. "New Harbor Plans are Suggested by Fisher," *Miami Herald*, February 4, 1920, p. 1.
3. Carl Fisher Papers, letter from Fisher to James Deering, August 6, 1919.
4. "Carl Fisher Urges Purchase of Lands on the Bay Shore," *Miami Daily Metropolis*, March 11, 1920, p. 1.

4. MEDIA AND ARTS

1. "Officers Carry Out Enforcement Prohibition Amendment in High-Handed and Autocratic Manner," *Miami Herald*, June 22, 1920, p. 1.
2. McGowan, P.H. "Southern City Blockaded 1st Time Since 1861," *Miami Herald*, August 11, 1920, p. 1.

5. HOTELS, INNS, APARTMENT HOUSES, AND RESTAURANTS

1. Mehling, Harold. *The Most of Everything*, p. 133.

2. Kleinberg, Howard. *Miami Beach*, pp. 71–74.
3. "Decorates Lunch Room With a Hundred Flags," *Miami Metropolis*, December 4, 1920, p. 2.
4. "Work Has Begun on Hotel Flamingo on the Beach," *Miami Daily Metropolis*, January 10, 1920, p. 1.
5. Carl Fisher Papers, letter from Carl G. Fisher to John LaGorce, December 4, 1920.

6. CASINOS AND BATHS

1. "Remarkable Panorama of Life at Beach Sunday," *Miami Metropolis*, June 15, 1920, p. 6.
2. "Beach Brevities," *Miami Metropolis*, July 2, 1920, p. 6.
3. Remington, Helona. "With Helona at Miami's Beaches," *Miami Herald*, August 16, 1920, p. 7.
4. "South Beach Night Life is Gay and Interesting," *Miami Metropolis*, September 21, 1920, p. 3.
5. "Season's Biggest Day Sunday at Casinoes Along Ocean's Shore," *Miami Metropolis*, December 6, 1920, p. 9.

7. THE SPORTING LIFE

1. "Cubans Win the Third Game of Polo Series," *Miami Herald*, March 16, 1920, p. 8.
2. "World's Best Polo Will be Played at Beach This Winter," *Miami Daily Metropolis*, October 9, 1920, p. 2.
3. "Professional Golfers Like the Course at Miami Beach," *Miami Metropolis*, February 4, 1920, p. 4.

8. DAILY LIFE IN MIAMI BEACH IN 1920

1. Roberts, Kenneth L. *Sun Hunting*, p. 183.
2. Editors of Time-Life Books, *The Jazz Age–The 20s*, p. 28.
3. Jack E. Davis, *The Wide Brim*, p. 44.

BIBLIOGRAPHY

BOOKS

Armbruster, Ann. *The Life and Times of Miami Beach*. New York: Knopf, 1995.

Bass, Jo Ann, and Richard Sax. *Eat at Joe's*. New York: Clarkson Potter, 1993.

Bramson, Seth. *Speedway to Sunshine*. Ontario: The Boston Mills Press, 1984.

Davis, Jack E. *The Wide Brim*. Gainesville: University Press of Florida, 2002.

Fisher, Jane. *Fabulous Hoosier*. Chicago: Henry Coleman and Company, 1953.

Fisher, Jerry M. *Pacesetter*. Fort Bragg: Lost Coast Press, 1998.

Foster, Mark S. *Castles in the Sand*. Gainesville: University Press of Florida, 2000.

Kennedy, Patricia. *Miami Beach in Vintage Postcards*. Charleston, SC: Arcadia Publishing, 2000.

Lavender, Abraham D. "Jews, Hispanics, Blacks, and Others in Miami Beach." Miami: Florida International University, 1992.

———. "The Post Office Comes to Miami Beach." *South Florida History* 27 (1999): 10–15.

Kleinberg, Howard. *Miami Beach: A History*. Miami: Centennial Press, 1994.

Lummus, J.N. *The Miracle of Miami Beach*. Miami: Miami Post Publishing Company, 1940.

Mehling, Howard. *The Most of Everything*. New York: Harcourt, Brace and Company, 1960.

Metropolitan Dade County. *From Wilderness to Metropolis*. Miami: Metropolitan Dade County, 1982.

Parks, Arva Moore, and Gregory W. Bush, with Laura Pincus. *Miami: The American Crossroad*. Needham Heights: Simon and Schuster, 1996.

Redford, Polly. *The Billion Dollar Sandbar*. New York: E.P. Sutton and Company, 1970.

Ridolph, Edward. *Biscayne Bay Trolleys*. Forty Fort, PA: Harold E. Cox, 1981.

Roberts, Kenneth L. *Sun Hunting*. Indianapolis: The Bobbs-Merrill Company, 1922.

Time-Life. *The Jazz Age—The 20s*. New York: Bishop Books, 1998.

Wynne, Nick. *Tin Can Tourists in Florida, 1900-1970*. Charleston, SC: Arcadia Publishing, 1999.

ARTICLES, INTERVIEWS, NEWSPAPERS, AND PERIODICALS

Fisher, Carl. Papers. Historical Museum of South Florida, Miami, Florida.

———. Letter to James Deering. August 6, 1919. Papers.

———. Letter to John LaGorce. December 4, 1920. Papers.

George, Paul. "Bootleggers, Prohibitionists and Police." *Tequesta* 39 (1979): 34–41.

Gutschmidt, Malvina Weiss Liebman. Interview by the author, September 16, 1997.

Line, Harger. "Business Men's Excursion to Havana Shows Possibilities of Trade With West Indies." *Miami Metropolis*, January 1, 1921.

McGowan, P.H. "Southern City Blockaded 1st Time Since 1861." *Miami Herald*, August 11, 1920.

Meloy, Olin. Interview by the author, November 9, 1997.

Miami Beach Chamber of Commerce. "Brief History of Miami Beach." Miami Beach: 1958.

Miami Beach City Council. Council Minutes for 1920.

Miami Daily Metropolis. "Carl Fisher Urges Purchase of Lands on the Bay Shore." March 11, 1920.

———. "Thrilling is Rescue of Girl Who Fell From Causeway." June 16, 1920.

———. "Work Has Begun on Hotel Flamingo on the Beach." January 10, 1920.

———. "World's Best Polo Will be Played at Beach This Winter." October 9, 1920.

Miami Herald. "Auto Tourists Migrate South." December 25, 1920.

———. "Cubans Win the Third Games of Polo Series." March 16, 1920.

———. "New Harbor Plans are Suggested by Fisher." February 4, 1920.

———. "Officers Carry Out Enforcement Prohibition Amendment in High-Handed and Autocratic Manner." June 22, 1920.

Miami Metropolis. "Beach Brevities." July 2, 1920.

———. "Decorates Lunch Room With a Hundred Flags." December 4, 1920.

———. "Professional Golfers Like the Course at Miami Beach." February 4, 1920.

———. "Remarkable Panorama of Life at Beach Sunday." June 15, 1920.

———. "Season's Biggest Day Sunday at Casinoes Along Ocean's Shore." December 6, 1920.

———. "South Beach Night Life is Gay and Interesting." September 21, 1920.

———. "Trial Trip of Beach Street Car Indicates Need of New Ruling." December 15, 1920.

Miami Herald, Miami Daily Metropolis, Miami Metropolis, and *The Weekly Miami Metropolis*, all issues for year 1920.

Remington, Helena. "With Helona at Miami's Beaches." *Miami Herald*, August 16, 1920.

Sanborn Map Company. Miami Beach, Florida. New York: Sanborn Map Company, 1918 and 1921.

INDEX